GUIDANCE MONOGRAPH SERIES

Shelley C. Stone

Bruce Shertzer

Editors

GUIDANCE MONOGRAPH SERIES

The general purpose of Houghton Mifflin's Guidance Monograph Series is to provide high quality coverage of topics which are of abiding importance in contemporary counseling and guidance practice. In a rapidly expanding field of endeavor, change and innovation are inevitably present. A trend accompanying such growth is greater and greater specialization. Specialization results in an increased demand for materials which reflect current modifications in guidance practice while simultaneously treating the field in greater depth and detail than commonly found in textbooks and brief journal articles.

The list of eminent contributors to this series assures the reader expert treatment of the areas covered. The monographs are designed for consumers with varying familiarity to the counseling and guidance field. The editors believe that the series will be useful to experienced practitioners as well as beginning students. While these groups may use the monographs with somewhat different goals in mind, both will benefit from the treatment given to content areas.

The content areas treated have been selected because of specific criteria. Among them are timeliness, practicality, and persistency of the issues involved. Above all, the editors have attempted to select topics which are of major substantive concern to counseling and guidance personnel.

Shelley C. Stone

Bruce Shertzer

MODERN MENTAL MEASUREMENT:

A HISTORICAL PERSPECTIVE

KATHRYN W. LINDEN
PURDUE UNIVERSITY

JAMES D. LINDEN
PURDUE UNIVERSITY

HOUGHTON MIFFLIN COMPANY · BOSTON
NEW YORK · ATLANTA · GENEVA, ILL. · DALLAS · PALO ALTO

PREFACE

Fable, parable, and proverb abound in allusions to tests of one kind or another. The wheat is separated from the chaff; the sheep are divided from the goats; the strong are set apart from the weak; and the wise are welcomed to the feast, while the foolish and improvident are allowed to remain in the outer darkness with their unfilled lamps. It is a far cry from the tests referred to in ancient lore to the scientific tests which, within the last decade, have found a permanent place in the schools of our country. But the fact remains that testing is not new, and that tests of intelligence are old and tried devices. For an adequate understanding of modern tests and their purpose, some knowledge of their evolution is necessary. (Peterson, 1925)

Although this statement was written more than forty years ago, it is as appropriate today as it was when Peterson included it in his introduction to *Early Conceptions and Tests of Intelligence*. For an adequate understanding of modern tests and their purposes, to say nothing of their proper uses, knowledge of their evolution is necessary. To the authors' knowledge, all major texts now published in the area of tests and measurements fail to provide more than a sketchy outline of the heritage of modern mental measurement. In part, this is the case because the space limitations afforded most authors prohibit the inclusion of much historical material in light of the weighty body of valuable technical information that most authors agree must be presented in such books. As two former high school history teachers, the authors have been distressed for some time by this state of affairs. They have been pleased to note a reawakened interest in the historical antecedents of several facets of scientific psychology. The recent establishment of a History of Psychology division in the American Psychological Association may attest to this current interest. Moreover, in the last year or so, they have been encouraged by the publication of several books and articles dealing with historical matters in the fields of education and psychology. However, the authors remain unaware of the publication of any updated historical account exclusively devoted to mental ability testing.

The series of which this monograph is a part afforded the authors an opportunity to try their hands at writing a brief but relatively thorough account of the heritage of mental measurement. Initially they intended to include material relevant to all types of tests. However, the finite limits allowed suggested that this would be unwise because only the most superficial account could be presented. It was decided to limit the content of this monograph to mental ability testing because of its wider use and to leave to another time and place an effort to trace the history of other types of tests, such as those used for the assessment of interests or personality.

This monograph presents material in three major sections. The first section traces the international origins of modern mental measurement. The second deals with mental measurement in America from the turn of the last century to the close of World War I, while the third section presents developments that have occurred since World War I. A brief fourth section serves as an epilogue to the other three. In it, certain suggestions are made regarding the implications that the past and present hold for the future of mental measurement. Selected references and a relatively comprehensive list of educational and psychological histories are included at the end of the monograph. The scope of this monograph is limited, but the authors trust that the content is adequate to provide test consumers with a better understanding and appreciation of the heritage of the mental ability measures they employ.

The authors dedicate this monograph to those who in the past have contributed to the growth of mental measurement as it exists today. Furthermore, they acknowledge their indebtedness to those who have recorded this history for another day, especially E. G. Boring and J. M. Reisman, whose writings have served as a guide to the writing of this manuscript. The authors also commend Mrs. Dorothy Taylor for her faithful service in typing the many revisions of this manuscript. Finally, the authors thank one another for the support and encouragement each has provided the other. Without this mutual support and encouragement, time would not have been found nor would effort have been expended to formalize the account that follows.

K. W. L.

J. D. L.

CONTENTS

EDITORS' INTRODUCTION

This monograph presents a contemporary history of ability measurement. It is current history because virtually all of those who created and participated in the historical events described lived and worked during the past fifty to seventy-five years. Indeed, many of them are still living. While the authors correctly point out that the desire and some efforts to assess human abilities have existed for centuries, meaningful implementation of that desire has occurred in fairly recent times.

The history and progress of both psychology and education would be markedly different if the extremely creative and productive individuals whose achievements the Lindens have chronicled had pursued other ends. The Lindens have richly documented their account and will provide upon request specific page citations for quotations referenced in the text.

Historians generally agree and, indeed, most base their professional existence on the tenet that knowledge of the past contributes to an understanding of the present and future. This tenet applies in a technical area, such as the field of ability measurement, as well as to the history of nations or mankind. The content of the brief but thorough history of a technical field provides its readers with background information essential to a comprehension of man's efforts to quantify, measure, evaluate, and assess that which enables men to achieve and accomplish — mental ability.

Shelley C. Stone

Bruce Shertzer

1

National Antecedents

At various periods of history, English legal writers have attempted to formulate tests for determining the mental status of persons either charged with a crime or otherwise under the observation of the law. Fitzherbert (1470–1538) proposed that the capacity of an alleged idiot to count twenty pence, to tell his age, or to identify his father and mother should be used as a test of mentality. Nearly a century later, Swinburne (1560–1623) suggested that the person charged or held should be examined to see whether he could measure a yard of cloth or name the days in the week. In the seventeenth century, the legal test proposed to determine responsibility for a crime was the level of understanding of a child fourteen years of age.

About this same time, European philosophers questioned whether psychical conditions and experiences could be measured in exact or mathematical terms. The then standard legal tests for mental unsoundness certainly were unable to measure accurately the mental state of an individual. Malebranche (c. 1675) had denied that mental states could be measured. Later, both Plouequet (c. 1763) and Kant (c. 1786) agreed. On the other hand, Wolff advocated a "science of psychometry" and Eberhard (c. 1776 and c. 1786) believed that "a mathematics of the soul" could be devised. By the early nineteenth century, while Galuppi (c. 1819) disagreed, Eschenmayer (c. 1822) recognized the possibility of "psychical" measurements.

The history of the last seventy-five years has justified the beliefs held by Wolff, Eberhard, and Eschenmayer. During this period of time, formal techniques of mental measurement have been developed scientifically and are widely used today. People in many lands have contributed to this achievement. To a large extent, these contributions, some of which predate this period, tend to reflect specific national characteristics: Spanish, German, English, American, and French.

Un Esfuerzo de Primero

Juan Huarte (1530–1589) may have been the first man to suggest formal mental testing (Roback, 1961). Huarte was a Spanish physician, probably of Basque origin, who was interested in practical questions that were essentially psychological in nature. An English translation (1698) of Huarte's 1575 book, *Exámen de Ingenios,* was titled *The tryal of wits, discovering the great differences of wits among men and what sorts of learning suits best with each genius.* From this title, it appears that Huarte's purpose was to guide youth and advise parents on the aptitude of their children. Writing nearly four hundred years ago, Huarte observed:

> All the ancient philosophers have found by experience that where nature disposes not a man for knowledge, 'tis in vain for him to labor in the rules of the art. But not one of them has clearly and distinctly declared what that nature is, which renders a man fit for one, and unfit for another science, nor what difference of wit is observed among men, nor what arts and sciences are most suitable to each man in particular, nor by what marks they may be discerned, which is one of the greatest importance. (Roback, 1961)

The first edition (1500 copies) of *Exámen de Ingenios* was published by the author himself. This book became a best seller. Twenty-seven editions in Spanish, twenty-four in French, seven in Italian, five in English, three in Latin, two in German, and one in Dutch were published subsequently. A facsimile of the old English translation of this work recently has been published (Roback, 1961).

Huarte examined the concept of intelligence and invested the term with what today might be called *productive imagination.* He viewed the characteristics of intelligence to be: (1) docility in learning from a master; (2) understanding and independence of judgment; and (3) inspiration without extravagance. As was true of others of his day, Huarte was preoccupied with all sorts of ancient hypotheses in regard to the humors and made much of the difference between the moist and the dry, and the cold and the hot. Huarte tried to reason and weigh conclusions. He attempted to explain differences between man and man, and between one nation and another, in terms of the proportion of heat and moisture in the organism. Despite his dependence upon ancient ideas, Huarte may be regarded as one of the enlightened men of his age who inaugurated the study of differential psychology and who foresaw the applications of intelligence testing.

Der Wirkliche Anfänge

The first of the modern specialties in science emerged in the realm of the physical sciences and mathematics during the late Middle Ages in Western Europe. The biological sciences evolved as separate disciplines perhaps 150 to 200 years later than did chemistry, mathematics, and physics. By the year 1800, most Western European scholars were schooled rigorously in philosophy, science, and mathematics. In the universities of the countries known today as Germany, Austria, Czechoslovakia, and Poland, there emerged a group of these men who, for their time, were a rather strange breed. Representative of a variety of scientific emphases and specializations, these individuals turned their attention to a new realm of exploration. Their interests were neither specifically in the realm of physics or chemistry, nor specifically in the realm of biology or physiology. Instead, they were interested in the scientific twilight zone between physics and physiology. Specifically, they were interested in the interaction between the stimuli of the physical world and the responses produced by living animal organisms. In other words, they were interested in behavior, especially human behavior. This interest provided the basic foundation from which modern experimental psychology has been developed.

During the first quarter of the nineteenth century, it was recognized that people differ from one another in their observations of the same event and that one individual will differ within himself across a series of observations. Moreover, it was believed that such individual differences, both between and within individuals, could be accounted for and measured. In 1809, an astronomer named Gauss, who was director of the Göttingen observatory, described a theory concerning errors of observation. In the next decade, Bessel (1784–1846), an astronomer working at the Königsberg observatory, began to investigate the personal difference between the observations of two astronomers and ultimately represented the difference as an equation (c. 1823). Bessel's investigations were prompted initially by his examination of the reason for the discrepancy between the star passage observations of Maskelyne and those of his assistant, Kinnebrook, at the Greenwich Observatory in England in 1795. He went further to establish the fact of variability among the observations of single individuals. Bessel's discovery came to be called the "personal equation" and led astronomers to identify personal equations and to correct for them (Boring, 1950).

Interest quickly developed concerning the psychophysiological explanation of personal differences and then focused upon speculations about the threshold of awareness, or *absolute limen,* i.e., that point at which a sensory stimulus first comes into awareness. Prominent among the early pioneers in this work was Ernst Weber (1795–1878), a German physiologist at Leipzig. Weber's principal findings dealt with the size of the *difference limen* at various levels of stimulation and yielded the principle that the just noticeable difference (JND) in a stimulus bears a constant ratio to that stimulus. It was Gustav Fechner (1801–1887) who gave Weber's empirical relationship mathematical form and named it "Weber's Law." Moreover, it was Fechner in whose hands the rising interest in human judgment became the cornerstone for modern psychological measurement (Nunnally, 1959).

When only 16 years of age, Fechner went to the University of Leipzig where he took his degree in medicine and then remained teaching and doing research until his death at the age of eighty-six. Although most of his teaching and research was based upon work in physics, Fechner was very interested in philosophy, and his speculations concerned the presence of conscious awareness in all living things, even in inanimate objects. These metaphysical speculations were incorporated in numerous pamphlets which were printed under the pseudonym, Dr. Mises.

Fechner attempted to verify his metaphysical beliefs through scientific experimentation utilizing studies of human judgment, particularly the JND, as his starting point. He based his research upon the postulate that, although sensation cannot be measured directly, it is legitimate to ask a subject directly whether a sensation is present or not and whether one sensation is more intense than another, a postulate that remains the logical basis of psychophysics. It was in this context that Fechner developed the law which he called "Weber's Law" (Boring, 1950).

In the course of Fechner's long program of experimentation, which he termed psychophysics, three major psychophysical methods of measurement and their related mathematical formulations were developed that still are basic to much psychological research today. Moreover, the general problem of measurement was assessed and mathematical procedures of analysis were formulated. Fechner's experiments dealing with visual brightness, with lifted weights, and with tactual and visual distances have become classics in the field of experimental psychology. Appearing in 1860, Fechner's *Elemente du Psychophysik* received enough attention from the academic world to give it a basic position in the new psychology and to stimulate immediate research activity and criticism.

For the next twenty years, the *Psychophysik* was the center of the attacks and criticisms that raged around Fechner and his mathematical theories. Fechner formally replied to these critical attacks in his *Revision der Hauptpuncte der Psychophysik* (1882), his last important work, although he published a half dozen more psychophysical articles before his death in 1886. While Fechner never was able to prove the philosophical beliefs to which he turned his attention periodically, he successfully demonstrated how the logic and methods of science could be utilized in psychological measurement, and ultimately became recognized as the founder of experimental psychology.

Even though Fechner "set experimental quantitative psychology off upon the course which it has followed" (Boring, 1950), the German psychologist whose ideas and practices were to have greater impact upon mental measurement was Wilhelm Wundt (1832–1920). Taking his doctorate in medicine at Heidelberg in 1856, Wundt quickly focused his interest upon physiology and then moved toward merging this interest with a growing appreciation of psychology. In 1858, he completed the first section of his *Beiträge zur Theorie der Sinneswahrnehmung* (the entire book was published in 1862), which expressed Wundt's early ideas about experimental psychology. By 1867, he had established formally a course at Heidelberg which was called "Physiological Psychology." Wundt's lectures for this course were incorporated into a book, the *Grundzüge der Physiologischen Psychologie* (1874), "the most important book in the history of modern psychology" (Boring, 1950), which later was revised and expanded into five more editions. A sixth and final three-volume edition contained 2,353 pages and was issued between 1908 and 1911. From 1853 to 1920, Wundt produced 491 items of writing containing a total of 53,735 pages (Boring, 1950).

In 1875, Wundt went to Leipzig, where he was given space for conducting experimental demonstrations in conjunction with his lectures. Four years later, in 1879, he founded the first psychological laboratory that was officially recognized as such by a university administration. To Wundt in his laboratory at Leipzig came the men who were to become important in the subsequent history of mental measurement: Kraepelin, Külpe, and Meumann in Germany; Angell, Cattell, Hall, Judd, Munsterberg, Scripture, Titchener, and Witmer in the United States. The work of the Leipzig laboratory essentially was aimed toward the formulation of generalized descriptions of human behavior. Uniformities rather than differences in behavior were the focus of attention. The fact that one individual reacted differently from another when observed under identical conditions was regarded as error or "the personal equation." The presence of such error, or individual variability, rendered the generalizations of human behavior to be approximate, rather than exact.

The nature of the problems studied at Leipzig and in the other German laboratories largely concerned sensitivity to visual, auditory and other sensory stimuli, and simple reaction time. The experimental methodology emphasized the need for rigorous control of the conditions under which the observations were made. The importance of making observations on all subjects under standardized conditions was demonstrated vividly, and such standardized procedures eventually became one of the special characteristics of psychological tests.

The importance of the accomplishments of Fechner, Wundt, and other early German scientists of behavior is not based upon the factual information they determined or the theories they developed. Most of what they thought, wrote, and professed has been superseded by the psychological research of the last 80 years. The *methods* of these men are the legacy they left modern psychology and measurement. They demanded respect for precision, accuracy, order, and reproducibility of data and findings. This heritage is the basis of modern demands for objectivity, reliability, and validity of mental measures.

The King's English

The founder of individual psychology, i.e., the psychology of human differences, was Sir Francis Galton (1822–1911), a gentleman-genius, an accomplished scholar, and an eminent scientist. Galton's family had been wealthy and prominent in England for generations. Perhaps because of a history of genius in his family, Galton became greatly interested in heredity, especially the hereditary aspects of genius. He was influenced by Charles Darwin, his first cousin. Galton's interest in heredity was tied closely to his cousin's theory of evolution and natural selection, or survival of the fittest. Being concerned with the problem of mental inheritance, he was interested, of necessity, in individual ability and achievements. Galton's first major investigation of mental inheritance was published under the title *Hereditary Genius* (1869), a careful biographical study of the tendency of genius to run in families. This book also represents the beginning of Galton's influence on statistical work with respect both to data collection and to methods of the statistical treatment of data.

During the next fourteen years, Galton's concern with the measurement of human faculties grew, continued to be focused on the problems of human evolution and eventually culminated in his *Inquiries into Human Faculty and its Development* (1883). This famous book has been regarded by many as the beginning of scientific individual psychology and mental tests. Intelligent selection of the more fit among the human species demanded, in the first place, a survey of available human assets. Combining his knowledge of statistics and interest in intelligent selection, Galton invented the *test* by which measurements of a single individual could be made easily and quickly. The test as an experimental method was characterized by its brevity and by its utility for sampling a large number of persons, in contrast to the elaborate psychophysical procedure of German psychology, which was conducted as an exhaustive analysis of single mental phenomenon involving a few subjects considered to be typical of all people. However, the simple mental tasks with which Galton experimented were primarily psychophysical in nature, just as were the mental phenomena studied by the Germans.

In 1884, Galton established the Anthropometric Laboratory at the South Kensington Museum in London. For the most part, Galton and his associates experimented with such simple mental tasks as discriminating between two weights, two colors, or two sounds, the speed and accuracy with which a subject could cancel all the "A's" on a page of printed material, color-naming, and associating as many words as the subject could with a particular stimulus word. Various kinds of apparatus necessary for these mental tests were invented by Galton. Data were recorded for some 9,337 persons during the six-year life of the laboratory. No really important generalization concerning individual differences appeared from the data collected, for the tests were too brief and the sample was too small and lacked representativeness. The Anthropometric Laboratory, nonetheless, was an important cornerstone of the movement to measure mental ability.

It was during the life of this laboratory that Galton first worked out the method of statistical correlation, although the idea had been forming in his mind for some years. Statistics had their historical beginning in the work of the Belgian mathematician, Adolph Quetelet (1796–1874), who was the first person to apply Laplace's and Gauss' "normal law of error" to the distribution of human data, both biological and social. The "normal law," originally developed in connection with the theory of probabilities in games of chance, had been used by Gauss to express errors in observation. Quetelet found that certain anthropometric measurements, such as the heights of men in the French army, were distributed in approximate accordance with this normal law, the bell-shaped probability curve. He assumed that human variation might be regarded as if it occurred when nature, aiming at an ideal, missed by varying degrees. Quetelet hypothesized that the position in the middle of the symmetrical curve, where the distribution of errors is smallest, reflects most closely the ideal that nature sought. The average man, *l'homme moyan*, according to Quetelet, thus appears as nature's ideal, and deviations away from the average appear as nature's errors in aiming at the ideal.

Galton first adopted Quetelet's use of the normal law in order to convert the frequency of the occurrence of genius into measures of the degree of genius. From the application of the normal law of error to the measurement of mental ability, Galton moved on to the concept of statistical correlation, a concept derived from his principle of "regression toward mediocrity" that appears in the phenomenon of inheritance. It was Karl Pearson (1857–1936), however, an associate of Galton, who provided the exact mathematical formulation for the theory of correlation (1904, 1912). Pearson and Galton established statistical investigations of psychological problems as a fundamental method in psychology.

An American Accent

Credit for establishing the foundations of mental measurement in the United States must be given to James McKeen Cattell (1860–1944). The son of a university president, Cattell grew up in a typical academic home and graduated with honors of many kinds from Lafayette College in 1880. In those days, bright young men who intended to make a career for themselves in the academic world wanted to obtain a status Ph.D. If a young man really wanted a first-class degree, he went to Europe to earn that degree. Thus, in 1880, Cattell went abroad for two years to study at Göttingen under the psychologist Lotze and at Leipzig under Wundt. It was during this time that Cattell was thoroughly and deeply influenced by the German interest in human capacities and the German attitude toward precision. Cattell then returned to the United States for a year's study at Johns Hopkins University.

In the days of 19th century Europe, the relationship between professors and graduate students was intimate. Graduate students came singly or in twos to study with a particular man. The arrangement was made via correspondence long before the student arrived at the university. Cattell, however, bypassed this usual approach upon his return to Leipzig in 1883. When paying his respects to the master, Cattell "informed Wundt in *ganz amerikanisch* fashion that he needed an assistant and that he, Cattell, would be it" (Boring, 1950).

For approximately three more years (1883–1886), Cattell studied and did research with Wundt. Wundt was committed to the pursuit of laws to explain and predict general human behavior. However, Cattell wanted to study differences among individuals, not their similarities. In spite of the heretical nature of Cattell's interest, Wundt permitted him to investigate individual differences in reaction time. Excitement over the reaction time experiment as a tool for mental measurement was then at its height. Combining a conventional interest in reaction times with an unconventional interest in individual differences, Cattell published more than half a dozen articles, several of which have become classics, prior to the completion of his dissertation in 1886.

After stopping briefly at Cambridge University, Cattell returned to America and took a position as a lecturer at the University of Pennsylvania and Bryn Mawr College for the academic year beginning in the fall of 1887. Returning to England the following year, he accepted an appointment as a lecturer at Cambridge University. For several months he taught, conducted some experiments on color, and generally impressed his English colleagues, as he had Wundt, with his American vim and vigor. It was during this time that he first came in direct contact with Sir Francis Galton. As a matter of fact, Cattell's major purpose in returning to England was to meet Galton; his teaching job merely paid his bills. Galton and Cattell quite independently had developed concern for the problems of individual differences. The similarity of their views drew them together.

From associating with Galton and his young and brilliant colleagues, such as Karl Pearson and Charles Spearman, Cattell became familiar both with the rudimentary kinds of mental tasks with which Galton had been working and with the new statistical techniques that had been applied to the measures of these mental tasks. Cattell returned to America determined to become a leader in the study and measurement of individual differences. For the next three years (1888–1891), Cattell was Professor of Psychology at Pennsylvania and established the psychological laboratory there. His appointment as Professor of Psychology was the first of its kind. Nowhere had anyone held such an appointment before; Wundt, for example, occupied the chair of philosophy at the University of Leipzig.

Cattell now devoted his attention to promoting mental testing. The term *mental test*, invented by Cattell, first appeared in his article entitled "Mental Tests and Their Measurements," which was published in *Mind* (1890). Reflecting both Galtonian and Wundtian influences, Cattell wrote:

> Psychology cannot attain the certainty and exactness of the physical sciences unless it rests on a foundation of experiment and measurements. A step in this direction could be made by applying a series of mental

tests and measurements to a large number of individuals. The results would be of considerable value in discovering the constancy of the mental processes, their independence, and their variation under different circumstances. Individuals, besides, would find their tests interesting and, perhaps, useful in regard to training, mode of life or indication of disease.

In general, Galton approved of what Cattell had to say. However, in an addendum to this article, Galton criticized Cattell for neglecting to mention the importance of what today would be termed test validity.

Meanwhile, A. Oehrn, Emil Kraepelin's student at Heidelberg, had worked out a set of tests for which he had divided mental capacities into four types: perception, memory, association, and motor functions. These tests were utilized in Oehrn's investigation (1889) concerning the interrelationships of complex psychological functions. This investigation probably was the earliest actual experiment in mental ability correlation. Somewhat later, Kraepelin himself (1895) devised a long series of tests designed to measure what he regarded as basic mental functions. Primarily interested in the clinical examination of psychiatric patients, Kraepelin utilized simple arithmetic operations in his tests which were designed to assess practice effects, memory, and susceptibility to fatigue and distraction.

Shortly after the publication of Cattell's now classic 1890 article, Joseph Jastro developed a set of fifteen tests for use with students at the University of Wisconsin (1892), which he later demonstrated at the Columbian Exposition in Chicago in 1893. Hugo Munsterberg at Harvard University prepared fourteen tests for use with school children which included tests of reading, verbal association, memory, and simple arithmetic operations (1891). Franz Boas (1891) compared school children's test results with teachers' estimates of their pupils' mental alertness. Boas' findings revealed little relationship between test scores and teachers' ratings.

In 1891, Cattell moved to Columbia University where he founded a new laboratory and remained its director for the next 26 years (1891–1917). In the 1890's, Columbia University was a mecca for American educators. A person seeking a status degree in professional education went to Columbia University, just as someone who sought a status Ph.D. in a scientific area went to Europe. The Columbia laboratory proved to be the most important single factor in promoting Cattell's influence on mental ability testing in the United States.

Using a battery of mental tests selected from those he had enumerated in his classic 1890 article, Cattell collected data from Columbia University freshmen in 1893 to initiate the very first study concerned with the prediction of academic success. His plan was to store these data until his freshman subjects had become seniors and then to correlate these predictor measures with the criterion measure of senior grade-point-average. His prediction, of course, was that his freshman mental measures would be indicative of the degree of academic success exhibited by these students as Columbia seniors.

During the four-year interim between the time he began his study and the time the final data were available, Cattell informed the educators who came to him to be taught psychology that a method had been devised for evaluating mental ability and predicting academic achievement. The educators saw the tremendous value such a method would have in terms of planning for the individual and in helping to facilitate the total program of the school. They listened enthusiastically to the master who promised so much.

While Cattell was waiting for the four years to pass, J. A. Gilbert investigated the mental and physical development of 1200 school children (1883, 1897). As Boas had reported earlier (1891), Gilbert found chance relationships between pupils' scores and teachers' ratings of pupils' mental ability. However, his work was significant in that he endeavored to introduce some control over the selection of his subjects. Approximately fifty subjects of each sex at every age level from six to eighteen years were administered Gilbert's tests: visual and auditory acuity, speed of tapping, reaction time, and tests including anthropometric measurements. A comparison with teachers' ratings was made by drawing curves representing the average score at each age for pupils judged by their teacher to be bright, dull, or average.

Cattell's final data were obtained and analyzed by one of his first graduate students, Clark Wissler. Wissler's results (1901) were anything but supportive of the promises Cattell had made for four years. Correlations of the psychophysical measures with later measures of school achievement were absolutely nil. In retrospect, one can criticize Cattell's initial tests as irrelevant to criteria of academic success in college. Moreover, performances on these tasks were so alike that there was no possibility of any differentiation or prediction.

When Wissler's report of Cattell's work was published, the educators, who had waited eagerly for some demonstrable evidence that Cattell's techniques were as valid as he had promised they would be, concluded that Cattell's techniques did not work and his promises were false. As a consequence, for some time thereafter, educators disparaged testing and were extremely reluctant to consider that tests had any practical value for the school.

However, one test was developed before the turn of the twentieth century that did demonstrate a clear relationship with school achievement: a sentence-completion test devised and tried out by the German psychologist, Hermann Ebbinghaus (1897). Included with tests of arithmetic computation and memory span, the sentence-completion test was to become one of the most widely-used of the early mental tests. Ebbinghaus himself referred to it as a "simple, easily applied device for testing those intellectual activities that are fundamentally important and significant both in school and in life" (1897). The sentence-completion technique was used later by Wiersma in his investigations of individual differences, by Terman in his studies of stupidity and genius, by Krueger and Spearman in their correlational treatment of mental tests, and by Lipman and Wertheimer who expanded the sentence-completion test into a "diagnosis-of-fact" test (Young, 1923).

In contrast, Cattell's measures behaviorally were very basic, at the order of psychomotor reflexes or just slightly above. These low order mental measures were totally inadequate to predict the results of fairly complex, high-order integrated learnings. One of his critics, Stella Sharp, a student of Titchener at Cornell University, published an article in 1898 which pointed up these criticisms of Cattell's work and suggested that the orientation of a Frenchman, Alfred Binet, was to be preferred over that of Cattell.

Ils Parlèrent Français Aussi

To a large extent, concern for the deviant individual motivated the French contributions to mental measurement. Although it is perhaps unwise to stereotype various national groups, it is interesting to note that Germans tend to be stereotyped as being emotionally cold, yet efficient, orderly, concise, precise, and systematic. The concerns and developments of the German psychologists mirrored these stereotyped characteristics. The French, on the other hand, possess a national stereotype of being a warm, easy-going, and loving people who care about others. In any event, the French were among the very first to provide special care for individuals who deviated from the ordinary person.

Specifically, the French were concerned about individuals who were mentally retarded, or emotionally or socially maladjusted. It was in France that the first schools for the mentally retarded were established. In France the first widespread humane treatment of mental hospital patients was provided, and the first developments in the rehabilitative treatment of delinquents and criminals were made. The first known test of intelligence was a French product.

Interested in differentiating between mental deficiency and mental illness, Jean Esquirol (1772–1840), a French physician, not only made explicit the distinction between the two mental conditions, but also proposed that there were several levels of mental deficiency (1838). He attempted to distinguish and classify mentally defective individuals on the basis of physical measurements, particularly the size and formation of the skull, but these attempts were unsuccessful. However, he was able to discern correctly the fact that the development and use of language would be valid psychological criteria for differentiating among levels of mental deficiency, behavioral criteria which Binet and Simon employed over half a century later in developing the first standard scale of intelligence. While Esquirol successfully identified the importance of language, he further believed that mental deficiency was incurable and, therefore, it would be a waste of time to attempt to educate such persons. This viewpoint was widely accepted by the medical profession and the general public and was enhanced further by the results of Jean Itard's unsuccessful attempts to educate the Wild Boy of Aveyron.

A young child, estimated to be about six years of age, was found running wild in the hilly forests of Aveyron in 1799. The authorities placed the boy in an institution established to care for mental defectives with which Esquirol and Itard were connected. Itard, a psychiatrist and colleague of Esquirol, believed that the mentally retarded could profit from training and asked that he be permitted to attempt to educate this child. For five years, Itard patiently labored to teach this boy and, although the results were not as rewarding as he had hoped, the boy did learn to dress himself and to read simple words. However, the child never learned to speak prior to his untimely death from an ordinary illness common to civilized children (Itard, 1962).

The fundamental significance of these efforts with the wild boy was noted by Itard's gifted pupil, Edouard Seguin (1812–1880). Having studied with both Esquirol and Itard, Seguin became an ardent protagonist of the doctrine that mentally defective individuals can be educated and that the success of the educator should be judged only in terms of the amount of improvement made by the learner and not judged by any absolute standard to be attained. Seguin put his doctrine to the test in 1837 when, at the age of 25, he established what became the first successful school devoted to the education of mentally defective children at the Hospice des Incurables in Paris. From all parts of the world, scientists and educators came to marvel at the progress made by the children in this school.

The ideas and methods of Seguin gained wide recognition not only as a result of his teaching and many public lectures but even more through his writings. He referred to his method of training as the "physiological method," which involved intensive training of low-grade mentally defective persons in sensory discrimination and in the development of motor control. He originated many of the "sense training" and "muscle training" techniques currently employed in the treatment of the mentally retarded. Among the educational devices he used was the *Seguin Form Board,* which required a subject to insert, as quickly as he could, blocks of various conventional geometric shapes into the corresponding recesses in a wooden board. Although Itard had originated and employed the form board concept in his training of the Wild Boy of Aveyron, Seguin refined and expanded the form-board technique that continues to bear his name. This and other techniques developed by Seguin were incorporated eventually into performance, or nonverbal, tests of intelligence, some of which are still in use today.

With Seguin's school as the model, the general attitude of the public toward the mentally defective changed to the belief that many, if not all, mentally defective individuals could learn to lead approximately normal lives in society, provided that appropriate educational methods are begun at a sufficiently early age. Except for one year spent at the Bicêtre in 1842, when he was invited to take charge of the division for the care and training of the feebleminded, Seguin continued his own school in Paris until 1848 when, because of political difficulties, he decided to leave France and make his home in America. Soon after his arrival in the United States, he established a training school for the mentally retarded at Vineland, New Jersey, the first school of its kind in this country. As he had done in France, Seguin stimulated widespread interest in the study and training of mentally defective children. In 1866, he published *Idiocy: Its Treatment by the Physiological Method,* a book which not only gained immediate attention but also continued to be recognized to the extent that it was reprinted and reissued some forty years later (1907).

Seguin, like Esquirol, maintained his efforts throughout his life to establish psychological criteria with which to differentiate among the levels of mental deficiency. The distinction between psychotic and feebleminded had been made by Jean Esquirol in 1838. However, this distinction had become significant only after reformers had campaigned successfully to provide separate institutions for the mentally ill and the mentally retarded. They then recognized the need to provide some objective means for the identification of the intellectually subnormal.

By 1900, a similar need was recognized in educational circles. The selection of children for special pedagogical programs could not be made sastifactorily on the basis of subjective impressions and appraisals. All too frequently, special classes and schools contained many children who should not have been placed in them; many other children who should have been so placed were not. The task of developing tasks for the purpose of securing objective appraisals of such children was to become a major interest of Alfred Binet, a French psychologist.

Born in Nice, Alfred Binet (1857–1911) originally had decided upon a career in law and had obtained a law degree from the Lycee Saint-Louis in 1878. However, an interest in research and the influence of Jean Charcot (one of Sigmund Freud's mentors) motivated him to study medicine and initiate a career in medical research (Reisman, 1966). In the early 1880's, Binet focused his interest upon psychological problems. At first, he emphasized theory building but also found time to devote some attention to thinking, hypnosis, and hysteria. With a beginning such as this, it is interesting to note that later Binet was criticized for a lack of an adequate theoretical perspective.

In 1889, with Henri Beaunis, Binet founded the first physiological psychology laboratory in France, at the Sorbonne. The following year he obtained a degree in the natural sciences and, in a limited way, initiated a program of research on intelligence, both animal and human. In 1894 he earned his doctorate in science with a thesis on the insect nervous system. When Beaunis retired from the Sorbonne the following year, Binet took over the direction of the laboratory. That same year, Beaunis and Binet founded the first French psychology journal, *L'Année Psychologique,* with Beaunis as its first editor. *L'Année* was the principal vehicle by which Binet published his research on intelligence. In 1897, he followed Beaunis' footsteps once again and assumed the editorship of this journal upon Beaunis' retirement from that post.

Early in his work on intelligence, Binet explored the relationship among intelligence, palmistry, and phrenology. He experimented with the same psychophysical measures as Wundt, Galton, and Cattell. However, early in the 1890's, Binet became convinced that, in order to study individual differences in intelligence, it was necessary to sample more complex mental processes. He recommended the construction of psychological tests which sampled judgment, memory, and imagination. Like Galton, Binet believed that the basic concept for individual psychology focused upon deviations from a population average. In addition, he wanted to know what relations existed between the various mental processes so that the development of one process might be predicted from knowledge of another. Furthermore, he thought mental tests should yield information about qualitative mental differences, as well as quantitative mental differences (Reisman, 1966).

In an article crucial to mental testing, Binet and Henri (1896) described a series of tests designed to measure attention, comprehension, memory, imagery, aesthetic appreciation, moral judgment, and visual space perception. For the next eight years, Binet continued to emphasize the importance of qualitative mental variables, particularly the influence of personality upon intellectual functioning. His studies made it clear that psychological measures were not absolute but ordinal in nature. Binet's most important writing of this period was a volume entitled *The Experimental Study of Intelligence* (1902).

In 1904, the Minister of Public Instruction in Paris appointed a commission to recommend procedures whereby mentally defective children might receive the benefits of an education. It was decided that special classes were to be formed, and, before a child could be admitted to these classes, an examination should be conducted to determine that the child could not profit from regular classroom instruction. In the hope that an objective basis might be used to make this determination, Alfred Binet and a young psychiatrist, Theóphile Simon (1873–1961), medical chief of the Insane Asylum of La Seine Inférieure, were commissioned to research this problem and to return recommendations to the Minister of Public Instruction.

The *Measuring Scale of Intelligence* resulted from their work (Binet and Simon, 1905a and 1905b). This scale was composed of 30 items arranged in order of increasing difficulty. Its score was simply the number of items passed. Binet claimed only that the scale provided a crude means of differentiating between those children who could function in the regular classroom and those children who could not. Although Binet and Simon also claimed that the essence of intelligence is sound judgment, they were forced to admit that many of the 30 items included in their 1905 scale did not test judgment.

The 1908 *Measuring Scale of Intelligence* was a more refined product (Binet and Simon, 1908). In it were 59 subtests, or tasks, grouped at age levels from three to thirteen years according to the percentage of children of a particular age who passed a given item. This percentage varied from 67 to 75. If a higher percentage passed an item, it was thought to be too easy for that age level; if a lower percentage passed an item, it was thought to be too difficult for that age. In short, an item had to be appropriate to the mental level of the modal child of a given chronological age. Moreover, to be acceptable, an item had to elicit this type of response from one age level sample and only from that sample.*

Having identified a pool of appropriate items, Binet and Simon then built these items into their 1908 scale by including a certain number of these items at each given age level. Binet had recognized that an indication of intellectual level, to be valuable, must represent measurements, not descriptions. For each of the age levels included in the test, the successful completion of a task at that level resulted in a certain amount of mental age credit being added to a subject's score.

When administering the test, Binet and his associates usually started with a level at which they felt the child could respond correctly to each of the tasks included at that level. For example, a seven-year-old child who appeared to be somewhat typical of seven-year-olds would be started at the five- or six-year-old level. The purpose in doing this was to identify a child's basal or foundation level of performance. Once this point was established, further tasks were presented at successively higher age levels until an age level was reached where the child failed all tasks. It was assumed that were the child to continue beyond this point he would not respond correctly to any further task. The mental age credits assigned to each task successfully completed were summed and added to the basal age score. The resultant sum was labeled a "mental age" score.

In essence, this mental age score was a measure of level of achievement. For example, a child who obtained a mental age score of eight years and six months was evaluated as having achieved at a level similar to the level achieved by the modal child who was chronologically eight years and six months of age. Binet warned that the scale not only measured intelligence but also measured knowledge gained from school and from the environment in general. He continued to stress the importance of qualitative variables that affect test results, e.g., the persistence and attention of a child while taking a test have an influence upon the score obtained.

Writing in 1912, William Stern, an Austrian, introduced the concept of the mental quotient, i.e., the ratio of a mental age score (level of accomplishment) to chronological age (1914). A mental quotient of *one* implies that the achievement of a child has progressed at a rate commensurate with his chronological age. To the extent that a mental

---

* "Binet and Simon did not know it, nor did hardly anyone else for that matter, but a pediatrician, S. E. Chaille, had constructed a series of tests for infants extending up to three years and had arranged them in order of age usually passed. Chaille's scale had been published in the *New Orleans Medical and Surgical Journal* in 1887." (Reisman, 1966)

quotient exceeds *one,* the inference may be made that the rate of intellectual growth must be more rapid than that which is typical of the modal child of the age in question. Conversely, to the extent that the quotient is less than *one,* the inference may be made that the child's rate of intellectual growth is slower than that of the modal child of his chronological age. At a second order of inference, the rate of intellectual development and intelligence have become associated. Rapid intellectual development has been accepted as behavioral evidence of a large capacity for mental growth. Conversely, slow intellectual development has been interpreted as indicative of a limited capacity for such growth.

In the spirit of the time, the nature of intelligence was viewed to be basically a genetic phenomenon. In spite of Binet's warnings, most persons viewed the measures associated with mental ability to be directly related to genetic endowment. A wide recognition of the impact of learning experience and cultural opportunity upon performance related to mental ability measures was delayed until a later period in the history of mental measurement.

Echoes

In short, mental measurement acquired method and respect for precision, accuracy, and prediction from the Germans. From the French, a concern for the identification of the deviant individual was added. The English interest in the study of mental inheritance led to the contribution of the basic statistical techniques used today to analyze the vast majority of behavioral and social science data.

However, mental measurement as it is known in the world today is primarily a product of the United States. Apparently an American crucible was required to take the contributions of Europe and blend them to yield a unified whole. The remaining sections focus upon this development.

2

From the Turn of the Century
to a World at War

Readin', 'Ritin', 'n' 'Rithmetic

Although mental measurement has found its application in military, industrial, and medical settings, by and large it was the schools that nurtured mental measurement in America through the early years of this century. The academic achievement test provided the prime motive for this nurture. Academic achievement testing was not new in the early 1900's, either in America or elsewhere in the world. History records that four thousand years ago a form of academic achievement testing was used in China to evaluate and assign civil service personnel. In 413 B. C., approximately 7,000 survivors of an ill-fated Athenian army in Sicily were thrown into quarries near Syracuse. For many of them, their lives and release from imprisonment depended upon ability to repeat verses of Euripides (Kelley, 1927).

The earliest record of the use of an achievement examination in a school in the western world dates back approximately to the year 1200, when the University of Bologna in Italy held the first oral examination for the Ph.D. degree. This was the only examination that a student at that time ever took. A student had but one chance to pass this examination, and it usually lasted about a week. European universities in those days used taverns as a base of operations, because the medieval tavern afforded both faculty and students a place where they could meet, talk, eat, and sleep. Consequently, the tavern was the place where the oral examination was held. It became a tradition for the student who was taking his oral examination to provide food and drink for everyone who attended (frequently all faculty and students), for as long as the oral lasted. It was not uncommon for these oral exams to turn into drunken brawls because of the surroundings in which they were held. This practice remained the only type of academic achievement test for 500 years. In 1700, at Cambridge University in England, the oral examination was extended downward to the master's degree level.

By the early nineteenth century, a formal plan of written examinations was common in Europe and, according to Horace Mann, partially adopted in some places in the United States (Mann, 1845b). In any event, the first written examinations in this country were introduced in Massachusetts by school examining committees in 1845, largely as a product of the desires, wisdom, and planning of Horace Mann (although Mann did not claim credit for inspiring the testing). These tests took the form of a comprehensive examination written at the end of high school to determine whether or not one graduated from high school. The various tests produced by the examining committees were administered to several hundred pupils in seventeen Boston schools and one in Roxbury, Massachusetts. The results were reported as percentages of correct answers on each test and in each school. The reports of the annual visiting committees of Boston were the first documented evidence of the use of comparative educational tests.

At the same time, it was fairly common to hold oral examinations at the end of grammar school; however, this practice was more a social affair than it was an academic evaluation. In those days, to graduate from grammar school was evidence that a person was fairly well educated. Each year, the elementary school teacher would publicly put his graduating pupils through their paces to show the community what the children had learned.

George Fisher

The pioneer work done in the field of scientific educational measurement is attributed to that of the Reverend George Fisher, an English schoolmaster. As early as the 1860's, Fisher had seen the need for standards in educational achievement and had anticipated later educational developments. E. B. Chadwick (1864) reported that Fisher had developed *scale books* for use in his school which contained numbers assigned to each degree of proficiency for given school subjects.

> The advantage derived from this numerical mode of valuation, as applied to educational subjects, is not confined to its being a concise method of registration, combined with a useful approximation to a *fixed standard* of estimation, applicable to each boy; but it affords also a means of determining the *sum total*, and therefrom the means of average condition or value of any given number of results. (Chadwick, 1864)

Fisher assigned a value of one to denote the highest amount of attainment and a value of five to denote the lowest amount of achievement for such subjects as writing, spelling, mathematics, navigation, scripture, grammar and composition, French, general history, drawing, and practical science. These scale books presented illustrations of various standard writing specimens and, in order to preserve the same standards of difficulty, the sentences were presented which were to be dictated for spelling, the numerical value of the spelling score being dependent upon the percentage of mistakes in writing from the dictated sentences. He also included sample questions for each area to serve as types of difficulty and item content for future reference.

For three decades, the Reverend Mr. Fisher's efforts seemed destined to be ignored. The scientific study of education was not possible until educators were brought to realize that human behavior could be quantified for scientific study and until statistical methods were developed for such investigations. The work of Sir Francis Galton contributed in large measure to both these ends.

J. M. Rice

A pediatrician turned psychologist became interested in the state of American education. J. M. Rice (1857–1934) found the practice of medicine unappealing and went to Germany to study psychology and pedagogy. In Germany, he came under the influence of the psychologists at Leipzig. Returning to the United States in 1890, Rice began to contrast American public schools with the German schools he had visited. In an article headed by the challenging title "Need school be a blight to child life?" Rice boldly asserted that "the entire public school system of the city of New York is conducted upon unscientific principles, not far in advance of those existing in the middle ages before the science of education came into existence" (1891). Spending six months visiting a large number of schools located from Boston to Minneapolis, Rice wrote a series of articles based upon his observations that were published in the *Forum* in 1892 and 1893. Only six school systems were relatively free from biting criticisms. Four of these school systems he actually praised: Indianapolis and La Porte in Indiana, the Lincoln School in Minneapolis, and the Francis W. Parker Cook County Normal School in Illinois. The major school systems of New York, Baltimore, Buffalo, Cincinnati, Chicago, and Boston were attacked without mercy.

Rice's criticisms of the schools centered primarily upon teaching methodology, and in line with this focus he undertook to demonstrate his premise that the teaching methods used in the schools did little to promote learning in children. Selecting spelling for study, Rice began "the first full-scale comparative 'experiment' ever done in schools and published" (Stanley, 1966). He devised three different spelling tests which he used to test approximately 33,000 pupils in grades 4–8 located in 21 different cities. The results and conclusions of this widespread investigation were reported in 1897 under the title "The futility of the spelling grind."

This article created an instant furor among American educators. One of the conclusions derived from this investigation suggested that the number of minutes spent in daily drill in spelling had almost no relationship to achievement in spelling. (In 1966, Englehart and Thomas calculated a correlation coefficient of $-.12$ for Rice's original data.) Rice's interpretations led educators and reviewers to unite in

> . . . denouncing as foolish, reprehensible and from every point of view indefensible, the effort to discover anything about the value of the teaching of spelling by finding out whether or not the children could spell. . . . The object of such work (drill) was not to teach children to spell, but to develop their minds! (Ayres, 1918)

To add fuel to an already brightly burning fire, Rice turned his attention to the study of arithmetic in 1902. He devised a set of arithmetic tests for grades four through eight which he then administered to nearly 6,000 pupils in 18 schools located in seven cities. The following year he prepared a language test in the form of presenting a story about which pupils were then to write a composition. Again, large-scale testing was his order of the day. More than eight thousand pupils in nine different cities wrote such compositions. These were scored by Rice himself using a five-point scale he had devised.*

Although all these efforts were crude by modern standards, Rice deserves recognition for his pioneer efforts in large-scale testing, ". . . his

---

* This concept in testing had been tried out in 1901 by the College Entrance Examination Board, who published an essay examination which became required of students seeking entrance into certain colleges and universities and which, with many modifications and revisions, is still in use today.

concern about reliable methods of measuring achievement in spelling, arithmetic and language, and his shrewd intuitive judgments about the learning process" (Englehart and Thomas, 1966). Although Rice was accorded considerable attention by E. L. Thorndike (10 pages in the 1903 edition of Thorndike's *Educational Psychology*), Rice's own role as a pioneer in educational measurement and research generally was not recognized and, "crucial as his survey was to the implementation of school reforms and his tests to the establishment of educational psychology, the man himself was quickly forgotten" (Graham, 1966). Had the man been somewhat less vitriolic in his attacks upon the American public school system of the 1890's and less vehement in his conclusions drawn from the results of his large-scale testing, Rice might have been accorded the role of eminence that his ideas of education, centered on the child and based upon psychological principles, and his large-scale investigations deserved. The tenor of the times, however, would not accept Rice as a leader of either educational thought or educational measurement. In the latter field, it was Edward L. Thorndike who came to be accorded the role of "father of educational measurement."

Edward L. Thorndike, et al.

Edward Lee Thorndike (1874–1949) was one of the many whose interest in psychology was stimulated by reading William James' *Principles of Psychology* (1890). James (1842–1910), America's senior psychologist, worked at Harvard. Consequently, it was to Harvard that Thorndike went for graduate study after taking his undergraduate degree at Wesleyan University. Having become interested in animal intelligence, Thorndike began experimentation with baby chicks but met opposition almost immediately from his landlady, who objected to the incubation and hatching of chicks in her tenant's room. Offering his aid to the young experimenter, James attempted to get him space in the psychology laboratory. When this attempt failed, James ". . . took Thorndike and his whole outfit into the cellar of his own home, much to the glee of the James' children" (Boring, 1950).

Although Thorndike felt indebted to the generosity of James and preferred to stay at Harvard while completing his doctorate, he had to earn a living. Therefore, when James McKean Cattell offered Thorndike a fellowship at Columbia in 1897, he left Harvard for New York, taking with him his two most educated chicks. Cattell was quite willing for Thorndike to continue his work with animal intelligence, which resulted in his doctoral dissertation *Animal Intelligence: an experimental study of the associative processes in animals* (1898). This study involved the use of a puzzle box for cats. The results firmly established Thorndike's first law of learning, the *Law of Effect*. The Law of Effect stipulated that the learner, to learn well, needs to obtain satisfaction from the learning experience. Thorndike formally stated the law somewhat later:

> Any act which in a given situation produces satisfaction becomes associated with that situation, so that when the situation recurs the act is more likely than before to recur also. Conversely, any act which in a given situation produces discomfort becomes disassociated from that situation, so that when the situation recurs the act is less likely than before to recur. (Thorndike, 1905)

Thorndike believed that the Law of Effect was operative in learning in addition to frequency of repetition, a principle identified by Ebbinghaus in 1885. When Thorndike formally named his discovery the Law of Effect, he also renamed Ebbinghaus' principle the *Law of Exercise*. Still another learning principle associated with the Law of Effect was proposed by Thorndike in 1905: his *Law of Readiness*. Readiness meant a preparation for action:

> When an action tendency is aroused through preparatory adjustment, sets, attitudes, and the like, fulfillment of the tendency in action is satisfying, non-fulfillment is annoying. (Hilgard, 1948)

With the publication of his dissertation on animal intelligence in 1898, Thorndike became established as the pioneeer of experimental animal psychology in the United States (Boring, 1950). (The dissertation was republished in 1911, together with other related studies, under the title *Animal Learning*.) In 1899, Thorndike was appointed an instructor in genetic psychology at the new Teachers College of Columbia University, where he remained until his retirement in 1940. He was made a full professor in 1906, and from 1922–1940 he served as Director of the Psychology Division of the Educational Research Institute. A very prolific writer, Thorndike produced more than 500 publications between 1898 and 1949.

Following the model established by Cattell and carried on by Robert Woodworth at Columbia University, Thorndike created an atmosphere for graduate study at Teachers College that was directed toward the study of what is useful to both society and the individual. This atmosphere is illustrated well in the words of Edna Heidbreder (written in 1924 and reprinted in Boring, 1950):

> . . . a graduate student in psychology cannot spend many weeks at Columbia without becoming aware of the immense importance in that atmosphere of curves of distribution, of individual differences, of the measurement of intelligence and other human capacities, of experi-

mental procedures and statistical devices, of the undercurrent of physiological thought. He discovered immediately that psychology does not lead a sheltered life; that it rubs elbows with biology, statistics, education, commerce, industry, and the world of affairs.

Upon joining the faculty of Teachers College, Thorndike was advised by Cattell to apply the animal intelligence techniques to children and young people. Thorndike accepted Cattell's suggestion and shifted his interests to human subjects. Two years later, in 1901, he published with Robert Woodworth a classic paper on transfer of training. Employed in this study were many of the tests that have been useful ever since. Becoming interested in statistics as well as human behavior, Thorndike in collaboration with Fox published a study in which several tests dealing with arithmetical operations were developed and used (Thorndike and Fox, 1903). The purpose of their investigation was to study relationships among the different arithmetical operations. That same year (1903), the first edition of Thorndike's pioneer *Educational Psychology* was issued.

A small 173-page book, *Educational Psychology* gained immediate attention from the school public, because it described the kinds of tests that were thought to be best for predicting educational success. Although yet somewhat suspicious as a result of Cattell's unsuccessful efforts only a few years before, many educators studied Thorndike's writings with some degree of optimism. With the publication of this brief book, educational psychology as a discipline became distinct from both child-study and pedagogy. The extent of educational psychology as a formal field of study was identified when Thorndike expanded his original writings on this topic into the three volumes that became a standard work in the United States: I. *The original nature of man* (1913a); II. *The psychology of learning* (1913b); III. *Individual differences and their causes* (1914).

Having introduced the field of educational psychology, Thorndike elaborated upon one particular area in educational psychology: the area of measurement. In 1904, he produced his classic *Introduction to the Theory of Mental and Social Measurements*, ". . . the book that first made the Galton-Pearson biometrical statistical methods readily available for the run-of-the-mill mental tester" (Boring, 1950). In addition to statistical methods, Thorndike discussed many of the principles upon which the construction of modern tests has been based. The revision of this book in 1913 contained the addition of concrete illustrations of these principles. Thus, although the educational measurement movement had been launched by Rice in the mid 1890's, it was Thorndike who provided the real impetus to modern educational measurement. "The test movement paralleled educational psychology, providing the latter with its most important tool" (Boring, 1950). By the use of the statistical procedures he had adapted from others (notably Galton and Pearson) and the testing principles he had established for the construction of tests, Thorndike and his students inaugurated the scientific study of educational achievement.

In December, 1909, Thorndike presented his *Handwriting Scale* before the meeting of Section L of the American Association for the Advancement of Science. The report of the derivation of this scale was published the following March in *Teachers College Record* (1910). Thorndike's *Handwriting Scale* was the first calibrated instrument for the measurement of an educational product. It made possible a quantitative description of an essentially qualitative product. Based upon the theorem that differences in quality are equal when they are noted equally often by competent observers, Thorndike secured a set of handwriting specimens that were rated consistently by experts as being qualitatively different. He arranged these specimens in order of increasing merit to form the scale. A pupil's handwriting sample was measured by matching it with the division of the scale the sample most closely resembled in general merit. The principles underlying the construction of this scale were applied to the area of English composition by M. B. Hillegas in 1912 and, with modifications and revisions, used by other workers for the measurement of both handwriting and English composition, notably L. P. Ayres, Daniel Starch, and M. R. Trabue.

Thorndike's *Handwriting Scale* set the stage for the rapid development of tests in many educational subjects and areas. By 1910 the furor raised by Rice over the state of American education had abated, and Thorndike's influence was strengthening a positive attitude toward mental testing. Educators were becoming more willing to attack rationally the problems in education created by factors such as: the expanding emphasis on individual differences initially recommended by Galton; the increasing enrollments in both elementary and high schools caused in part by the large influx of European immigrants to the United States; the continued progress of the industrial revolution with its accompanying increased need for skilled and professional workers; and the growing attention being paid to the educational philosophies of John Dewey and William James.

The work of Rice and the influence of Thorndike inspired C. W. Stone, one of Thorndike's students, to undertake the investigation of two questions in the field of arithmetic:

1. What is the nature of the product of the first six years of arithmetic work?
2. What is the relation between distinctive procedures in arithmetic work and resulting abilities? (Monroe, 1923)

To investigate these questions, Stone devised two tests, one on basic arithmetical operations and the other on reasoning. Published in 1908, Stone's *Arithmetic Test for the Fundamental Operations* and *Arithmetic Reasoning Test* were designed as a single test for grade six. Neither test was standardized when used in the original study, although the reasoning test was standardized later and was used extensively both in school surveys and by classroom teachers. In constructing his tests, Stone was more scientific than Rice had been in that weights were determined to more nearly equalize the units of the scale. Printed directions were provided for administering the tests and for scoring the test papers. Objectivity of the tests was effected by providing sufficiently detailed directions in order that different examiners would obtain approximately the same results in applying the tests to a group of pupils. Known popularly as "Stone's Standard Tests," their major contribution to educational measurement was that they became the basis for the experimentation of Thorndike-trained S. A. Courtis that resulted in the derivation of his *Arithmetic Tests Series A* (1909).

Assisting Stone with the administration of his tests to sixth graders, Courtis conceived the idea of giving the tests in all grades from one to twelve. He was interested in measuring the growth of pupils in arithmetic and in establishing norms for all grades. During the school year of 1907–08, Courtis administered Stone's tests to pupils in grades one to twelve but found the tests to be unsatisfactory for his purposes. Therefore, he devised his own *Series A* tests which were made available for use in September, 1909, and revised in 1911. The series consisted of eight tests: one test on the fundamental facts associated with each of the four basic arithmetic operations; a copying of figures test; two tests devoted to reasoning or the solving of problems; and a test including examples of each of the four basic operations. Courtis exercised a great deal of care in the construction of the tests, in the formulation of the directions and record blanks for their administration and objective scoring, and in their standardization. Measures of pupils' rate of work were secured by setting a time limit for each test. In his utilization of the variability of a defined group for interpreting individual test scores, Courtis promoted in educational measurement a concept that had been recognized originally by Galton (c. 1889), had been encouraged by Cattell and Spearman, and had been applied first to grade norms by Rice in 1897 (Kelley, 1927).

Courtis believed that tests should aid the classroom teacher in instructing pupils. By comparing the measures of achievement with the norms for the tests, a teacher could diagnose a pupil's educational needs. While Rice's interest in testing had been motivated primarily by school administration concerns and Thorndike's interest focused upon techniques of test construction, Courtis desired to establish tests as an aid to instruction. Results of the extensive use of the *Series A* tests by school teachers convinced Courtis that the tests were unsatisfactory in a number of respects. Therefore, he developed a new group of tests which he called *Series B* (1914). This series, the *Standard Research Tests in Arithmetic, Series B,* consisted of four tests, one on each of the fundamental operations with integers designed to measure both rate and accuracy of performance. The examples were relatively long and, within each test, all were the same size, e.g., each example in the arithmetic test consisted of three columns of nine digits each. Writing about the Courtis tests in 1913, Stone reported:

> The tests of Mr. Courtis are doubtless the best available . . . . They afforded means of measuring and interpreting results in the four fundamental operations and in simple reasoning. . . . Every teacher, whether she is following a particular or unique method or not, can and should utilize tests to determine the needs at the opening of the year or term, to determine progress during the year or term, and to measure losses during vacation.

Maintaining his conception of tests as instruments to aid the teacher, Courtis also developed an elaborate set of practice exercises in arithmetic that were ". . . the first of a new type of instructional materials . . . standardized, diagnostic, self-instructive and self-corrective" (Courtis, 1938). When these practice tests were placed on the market in 1912, their success was phenomenal. Thus, by seeing the need to provide children with experience in dealing with computational and reasoning tasks of the types he used in his standardized tests, Courtis inaugurated an adjunct program relating testing to curriculum. In addition to arithmetic, Courtis later developed standardized tests for several other school subjects.

In the 1910–1911 survey of the New York City public schools, tests were employed for the first time in a school survey to measure the achievement of pupils as a means of evaluating the effectiveness and efficiency of a school system. Among the tests employed in this survey were Courtis' *Series A* tests which were administered to more than 30,000 children. Courtis, a member of the survey commission, prepared the three-volume report of the findings and conclusions of this study. The Courtis tests also were employed in subsequent large-scale school surveys including those of Boston, Cleveland, Salt Lake City, and Bloomington and Gary in Indiana.

Among the many other Thorndike-trained Columbia Ph.D.'s who contributed to early educational measurement was B. R. Buckingham. Interested in the measurement of spelling, Buckingham developed a scale which represented a new type of measuring instrument (Buckingham, 1913). The difficulty levels of the fifty words selected for the scale were determined on the basis of the percentage of correct responses made by pupils in the various school grades. The words then were arranged in the scale in the order of their demonstrated difficulty levels. The scale also included approximately 125 supplementary words. The theoretical basis for Buckingham's test construction procedure was that the ability of a pupil may be measured by the level of difficulty he is able to reach on the scale. The scale itself was not published separately, because it was regarded primarily as experimental. However, Buckingham's principle of test construction was employed by L. P. Ayres for his *Spelling Scale* and by other educational measurement people in their construction of tests for several subject-matter areas, e.g., C. Woody in arithmetic operations tests, H. G. Hotz in algebra, V. A. C. Henmon and H. A. Brown in Latin, M. R. Trabue in language, and M. J. Van Wagenen in history. Buckingham's *Extension of the Ayres Scale* (1916) for use in grades two to nine was used widely in schools. This extension consisted of adding 599 words to Ayres' original spelling scale, primarily at the more difficult end of the scale. He also devised tests for arithmetic and other elementary school subjects.

Another strong influence responsible for the rapid development of the "movement for measurement" was the work of L. P. Ayres, yet another Thorndike product. In 1907, Ayres became the director of a newly-established division of the Russell Sage Foundation in New York City. The school survey work conducted by Ayres under the auspices of this foundation had "great effect in directing the minds of school people to the possibilities of measurement." (Ashbaugh, 1918) Among the major surveys directed by Ayres was the Springfield (Illinois) School Survey (Ayres, 1914). Having completed the Springfield survey, Ayres was invited by the Cleveland Foundation to direct a survey of that city's public schools (Ayres, 1915–16). It was in this survey that tests of reading were developed and applied for the first time on a large scale. W. S. Grey devised the standardized reading tests, both oral and silent reading. Other subject areas were assessed by either new tests constructed especially for the survey (e.g., *Cleveland Survey Arithmetic Tests*) or recently developed instruments (e.g., *Ayres Spelling Scale*). Known popularly as the "Cleveland survey tests," this package came to be employed in the school surveys of other cities, notably those of Detroit, Grand Rapids, and St. Louis.

In his role as director of the Russell Sage Foundation and of various school surveys, Ayres contributed to the dissemination of information concerning educational measurement through his numerous addresses to school personnel and to the general public. He developed writing and spelling scales that were employed frequently in the surveys and which, as a result, enjoyed widespread popularity in schools. The Ayres' *Handwriting Scale* (three-slant edition) published in 1912 represented ". . . an ingenious attempt to secure an objective index of the quality of handwriting" (Monroe, 1923). The criterion of quality was legibility of handwriting. Under controlled conditions, samples of pupils' handwriting were read, and an index of legibility was calculated from the average rate of reading. Studies using the scale revealed that it was not distinctly superior to Thorndike's scale. Moreover, Thorndike's scale construction was simpler than Ayres' method. For these reasons, the Ayres method was not followed by others who developed handwriting scales. Ayres himself altered this procedure in the subsequent editions of his instrument. His most significant contribution to test construction was a *Spelling Scale* (1915) for which he emphasized the importance of determining educational objectives as a prerequisite of test construction. This scale consisted of 1,000 words arranged according to difficulty level as determined by percentage of pupils who spelled a given word correctly.

The influence of Thorndike *et al.* was far-reaching. The results of the school surveys in major cities led school officials to take a closer look at school curricula. The first printed evidence of the relationship between research findings and curriculum appeared in the *Twelfth Yearbook of the National Society for the Study of Education* (1913), in which the use of tests in schools was advocated officially for the first time. School superintendents began to employ statistical methods in the analysis of school facts. Departments of education in universities developed courses of instruction in statistical methods for training administrators and technicians in educational research, and Thorndike's revised *Introduction to the Theory of Mental and Social Measurements* (1913d) was designed for use in such courses.

To promote the formal study of the work of the school, *bureaus of educational research* were organized by independent foundations, by city and county school systems, by state departments of public instruction, and by university centers under the direction of persons eminent in the measurement movement. Notable among the first city educational research bureaus were those established in 1914 by Baltimore and by Rochester, New York. The following year, similar organizations were established by the State of New York and by New York City, where E. A. Nifenecher served as director. In 1914, the operation of other bureaus was initiated in Boston under the leadership of F. W. Ballou, in Detroit under the direction of S. A. Courtis, and in Oakland, California, under the administration of V. E. Dickson. Kansas City completed the roster of these pioneer educational research bureaus when, in 1915, G. Melcher took charge of the new city bureau there.

The potential public service value of educational measurement also was recognized quickly by universities and stimulated the establishment of bureaus of cooperative research. In 1913, the University of Oklahoma formally organized its Bureau of Measurements and Efficiency, thus becoming the first of the university educational research centers. The Bureau of Cooperative Research at Indiana University, the Bureau of Educational Service at the University of Iowa, the Bureau of Educational Measurements at the University of Nebraska, and the Bureau of Educational Measurements and Standards at Kansas State Normal School were established the following year. Other colleges and universities followed these pioneers. Eventually the university cooperative research bureaus were to take over the major share of the educational research activities within their respective states. During the early days, however, private, local, and state bureaus maintained the primary lead in such activities. Additional aid to the measurement movement was provided by the U. S. Bureau of Education in the forms of printed bulletins, committee reports on standardized testing, and a general support of school surveys.

The development of research organizations had immediate impact upon the measurement movement as a whole. Service was rendered by making tests easily accessible to school personnel, by standardizing tests devised by others, and by constructing new standardized tests. Moreover, through their work, school administrators and teachers became acquainted with tests and testing, and many were trained in the use of tests. The sale and use of tests grew to unprecedented proportions:

> Last year (1916), of a single popular test, nearly 900,000 were used, and the annual sale of a few other tests runs well over 100,000 copies each. Nor is the use of tests confined to this country. Shipments are made to all quarters of the world. It seems quite probable, therefore, that the number of bureaus of research are destined to be greatly increased in the immediate future. (Ashbaugh, 1918)

Moreover, by 1918, W. S. Monroe was able to present and briefly review a partial list of 109 standardized achievement tests already on the market, including 84 tests designed for the elementary grades through grade eight and 25 for the high school level. For the elementary grades, tests of arithmetic and language led Monroe's list with 17 tests in each area, followed by silent reading (13), spelling (11), handwriting (10), geography (6), history (4), oral reading (4), music (1), and drawing (1). Tests in foreign language (11) outdistanced the other high school subject areas, which included seven algebra tests, three geometry tests, and one test each in history, physics, drawing, and physical training. (The most productive of the high school test authors was Cornell-trained Daniel Starch who devised tests for most of the secondary subjects, including algebra and geometry, the physical sciences, English, French, German, Latin, and Spanish.)

Presented in the same publication as Monroe's list of tests and standards (*Seventeenth Yearbook, National Society for the Study of Education,* 1918) was Edna Bryner's bibliography which contained 62 references on test theory and development, 357 references on tests and scales in school subjects, 23 references regarding uses of tests and scales in schools, 22 references on teacher measurement, 20 references for lists of tests and scales, 10 references concerning correlations between abilities, and 151 references on school surveys. All in all, this was dramatic evidence of the growth of educational measurement since Rice's explosive attack on America's schools less than twenty years earlier.

On the eve of World War I, mental measurement was recognized as the most important tool of educational psychology. Intelligence had become educational psychology's special area of study and Thorndike was its mentor. In 1918, Thorndike presented a basic tenet of faith in the value of testing in an article included in the *Seventeenth Yearbook, National Society for the Study of Education:*

> Whatever exists at all exists in some amount. To know it thoroughly involves knowing its quantity as well as its quality. Education is concerned with changes in human beings; a change is a difference between two conditions; each of these conditions is known to us only by the products produced by it — things made, words spoken, acts performed, and the like. To measure any of these products means to define its amount in some way so that competent persons will know how large it is, better than they would without measurement.

During the decade preceding World War I and for some time thereafter, Thorndike was the "oracle in educational statistical work, representing the multimodel view of intelligence and other personality components as against the unitary and bimodal theories" (Roback, 1961). No real challenge to Thorndike's position of influence was raised by anyone in America. However, across the Atlantic in England, Charles Spearman did have some things to say that initiated an academic dialogue which, from time to time, others carry on even to this day.

Dialogue at a Distance

Charles Edward Spearman

Charles Edward Spearman (1863–1945), an English psychologist who earned his Ph.D. on space perception under Wundt at Leipzig, was among the first psychologists to proffer an explanation of intelligence derived from empirical evidence. Inspired by Galton's work on statistical correlation, Spearman turned his attention in 1901 to the problem of finding out whether intellectual abilities are related to each other. His labors resulted in the now classic papers "The proof and measurement of association between two things" (1904b) and "General intelligence objectively determined and measured" (1904a). The latter paper introduced his "two-factor" theory of human capacity. In 1906, returning to England from further study at Leipzig, Wurzburg, and Göttingen, Spearman was made Reader at University College, London. He was advanced to the Grote Professorship of Mind and Logic in 1911. A chair as Professor of Psychology was created for him upon his retirement from the Grote professorship in 1928. From 1931 until his death in 1945, Spearman held temporary teaching posts in the United States on three different occasions.

Movement toward the more precise methods of standardizing tests and of calculating their results is represented in the early work of Spearman. In his 1904 article on intelligence, Spearman critically reviewed previous tests, outlined the major problems that should be studied, and indicated the techniques by which these problems might be attacked. Previous work was criticized on four points: (1) investigators had failed to use precise quantitative expressions to represent the degree of correlation between tests, or between tests and other measures; (2) the previous work did not include calculations of the probable error of the correlation; (3) certain irrelevant or falsifying factors which might produce misleading correlations were not eliminated; and (4) errors in observation were not taken into account. In short, Spearman emphasized the necessity of employing precise methods of calculation. Although the mathematical formula for calculating correlation had been determined by Karl Pearson (who had modified a previous method developed by the mathematician Bravais), Spearman presented two less complicated formulae for estimating a correlation coefficient: the *rank method* and the *footrule method*. He also emphasized the need to employ Pearson's formula for determining how reliable a correlation coefficient is, because both the number of cases studied and the size of the correlation coefficient itself affect the degree of confidence that may be placed in interpretations of the results.

In calling attention to the complexity of factors which affect a correlation coefficient, Spearman proposed that certain extraneous factors may influence the magnitude of this index — e.g., kinship between the individuals who are tested, differences or likenesses of the social class or age of such individuals, and differences in attitudes or abilities. He presented a formula for estimating what the true correlation would be if the influence of an irrelevant factor were removed. He also devised and presented a formula for determining what the relationship would be if the effect of errors in measurement were eliminated. The application of this latter formula has become known as the *correction for attenuation*. Furthermore, Spearman pointed out that the proper method for determining the accuracy of a test is to administer it twice to the same group and then to calculate the correlation (reliability coefficient) between the two sets of scores.

The fact that various measures of apparently different mental abilities consistently were found to be positively intercorrelated suggested to Spearman that the prevalence of these positive correlations must be due to the existence of a general factor, or capacity, common to all types of intellectual performance, and a specific factor for each different type:

> All branches of intellectual activity have in common one fundamental function (or group of functions), whereas the remaining or specific elements of the activity seem in every case to be wholly different from that in all the others. (1904a)

Spearman suggested that this general intellectual ability, General Intelligence, or simply *g*, is expressed in varying degrees in all mental functioning. To account for the finding that scores between various mental tests were not correlated perfectly, he assumed that, in addition to differences attributable to sampling error, various test situations demanded different degrees of general intelligence. In other words, *g* is more important than specific factors in determining an individual's responses on some tests; on other tests, a specific factor (*s*) is more important than *g*. Moreover, the nature of *s* varies from one test situation to another.

Spearman assumed that there was a host of specific factors which were independent of each other and were unrelated to *g*. Keenness of vision, for example, would depend chiefly on a particular specialized factor that would not be correlated either with other specific factors, such as keenness of hearing, or with *g*. These assumptions about the nature of intelligence, based upon empirical evidence of intercorrelations between tests, became known as Spearman's *Two Factor Theory of Intelligence*. To further substantiate this theory, Spearman undertook a series of studies of the hierarchical arrangement of coefficients of intercorrelation between tests. The first of these investigations was made in collaboration with B. Hart and was reported in the *British Journal of Psychology* (1912). Further evidence of the existence of some sort of general factor in mental tests was provided by the systematic fashion in which tests intercorrelated with each other.

Although Spearman was convinced that he had found the ultimate explanation of the nature of intelligence, other psychologists were not so certain. Thorndike sharply criticized the two-factor theory. Writing in 1913, he agreed with the general fact of positive correlation between intellectual traits but rejected Spearman's hypothesis that a single common factor is responsible for this correlation. Thorndike believed it was an error to suppose ". . . that some one function is shared by all intellectual traits, and that whatever resemblances or positive correlation the traits show are due to the presence in each of them of this function as a common factor" (1914). An early study by Thorndike and Woodworth on transfer of training (1901) had suggested the existence of specific abilities in intelligence, not one general ability. They had found that improvement in one subject-matter area rarely brought about equivalent improvement in another; e.g., improvement in Latin did not lead to corresponding improvement in mathematics. Hence, Thorndike held that this evidence contradicted Spearman's theory. In response to Spearman's interpretation of the systematic arrangement of the correlations among tests as evidence of the existence of a general factor, Thorndike (1914) countered with this statement:

> A table of the known degrees of relationship would abundantly confirm the statement that the mind must be regarded not as a functional unit, nor even as a collection of a few general faculties which work irrespective of particular material, but rather as a multitude of functions, each of which involves content as well as form and so is related closely to only a few of its fellows, to the others with greater and greater degrees of remoteness.

This interpretation of intelligence as a multitude of special abilities involving content as well as form appears to be a description of intelligence in terms of test behavior products. Moreover, Thorndike drew distinctions between classes of abilities, some of them more and others less intellectual. He also distinguished between abstract intelligence, social intelligence, and mechanical intelligence, i.e., the respective capacities for dealing with symbols, with persons, and with things. On the other hand, Spearman defined intelligence in terms of an analysis of the mental processes involved, irrespective of the content or form of the responses elicited by a test (Hart and Spearman, 1912). To explain the unity of intelligence indicated by statistical studies of mental tests, Spearman later proposed a quantitative principle intended to explain differences in degree of intelligence among different individuals:

> "G" measures something of the nature of an "energy" derived from the whole cortex or wider area of the brain. Correspondingly, the *s*'s measure the respective efficiencies of the different parts of the brain in which this energy can be concentrated; they are, so to speak, its "engines." Whenever the mind turns from one operation to another, the

energy is switched off from one engine to another, much as the power supply of a factory can be directed at one moment to turning a wheel, at the next to heating a furnace, and then to blowing a whistle. (Spearman, in Freeman, 1926)

Although the difference between the Thorndike and Spearman schools of thought was more apparent than real, the controversy persisted and became intensified by demands for capitulation from the proponents of one position to those of another. Thorndike himself finally grew weary:

> Of all the major participants in this dispute, Thorndike seemed to relish it least, and probably entertained the hope that such barren arguments would be put aside and everyone would go back to the work of being psychologists engaged in profitable research, rather than polemists. (Reisman, 1966)

Spearman, too, eventually desired to bring the dispute to a close. In his now classic book *The Abilities of Man* (1927), he suggested a compromise which he hoped (in vain) would settle the controversy once and for all. Meanwhile, in the United States, interest in the development of tests to assess mental ability was reawakened. Many psychologists worked long and hard at this task prior to World War I. Although they paid little attention to the theoretical foundations of the construct for which they labored, their products appeared to be more congruent with Spearman's g than with Thorndike's multiple abilities. One such psychologist was Lewis Terman.

The Assessment of Intelligence Revisited

Lewis Terman

Born and reared in south central Indiana, Lewis Terman (1877–1956) taught and served as principal for an Indiana township high school while attending college at Danville, Indiana, where he obtained three different undergraduate degrees. He went on to Indiana University in 1901 and obtained both the A. B. and the A. M. degrees within the next two years. Influenced by three psychology professors who had taken their doctorates at Clark University, Terman ". . . became fired with ambition to become a professor of psychology and to contribute something . . . to science" (Terman, in Murchison, ed., 1932). He chose Clark University for his doctoral work, where he studied under G. Stanley Hall and E. C. Sanford.

A great admirer of Galton, Terman became interested in studying precocious children and in using tests for his work with such children. Although his graduate studies were interrupted by pulmonary illness, he received his doctorate in 1905 with a thesis on mental tests. Terman then moved to California where he served as principal of a high school in San Bernardino for one year, followed by four years as Professor of Child Study and Pedagogy at the Los Angeles State Normal School. In 1910, he was invited by Professor Elwood Cubberley to join the faculty of Stanford University, an affiliation Terman maintained until his death in 1956. Throughout the years at Stanford, Terman's continued interest in the study of giftedness found expression in large research projects which he undertook with the aid of many assistants. Important among these projects were the *Genetic Studies of Genius,* published in five volumes from 1925 to 1959, with Terman as general editor of the series and as a principal author of all except Volume II, which was authored by Catherine M. Cox.

Before leaving Los Angeles for Stanford in 1910, Terman was urged strongly by psychologist E. B. Huey (another Clark Ph.D. who had worked with psychiatrist Adolf Meyer at Johns Hopkins University) to start work on a revision of the 1908 Simon-Binet Scale. Although H. H. Goddard, still another Clark product, had just translated the 1908 Simon-Binet Scale into English (1910) and had introduced it to America at the Vineland, New Jersey, Training School for Mentally Retarded Children, to Huey (1910) the Goddard revision seemed inappropriate for use with school children. Impressed by Huey's advice and given a light load and free range of courses in educational psychology by Cubberley, Terman immediately began an experimental study of the 1908 Simon-Binet Scale in collaboration with H. G. Childs, one of his graduate assistants. Their efforts resulted in the publication of the Terman and Childs' tentative revision of the Simon-Binet Scale in 1912. Of Binet himself, Terman later wrote:

> My favorite of all psychologists is Binet; not because of his intelligence test, but because of his originality, insight, and open-mindedness, and because of the rare charm of personality that shines through all of his writings. (In Murchison, ed., 1932)

Between 1910 and 1916, Terman's major research interest was centered upon his revisions of the Simon-Binet Scale. His approach was to check out the validity and accuracy of the Scale items just as Binet himself had done originally, but this time upon an American population. The final product was to be truly an American product adapted to American needs, and not merely an American translation of a French instrument. Terman accepted Binet's basic conceptual model of intelligence and Binet's principle of scaling. He did not, however, include Binet's items in his new revision unless they were found to be of diagnostic value when tried out and carefully tested on an American population. Many Binet items that were retained in the scale were modified greatly before being found worthy of inclusion. Moreover, many completely new items were added. Although the final instrument was essentially a brand new scale which bore only a surface resemblance to its predecessors, Terman named it the *Stanford Revision of the Binet-Simon Scale of Intelligence.*

Terman's scale was standardized upon approximately 1,000 children up to 14 years of age and 400 adults. It covered an age range from three years to a "superior adult" level. Terman was the first test constructor to realize the major importance of securing a representative sample of subjects for use in the standardization of a test. For the subjects in his standardization sample, he selected children who were within two months of their birthdays at the time of testing and who were attending schools in communities surrounding Stanford University that were judged to be average in terms of socioeconomic condition. Published in its final revised form in 1916, Terman's "Stanford-Binet" quickly became the most widely used individually administered scale of intelligence in the United States, much to Terman's surprise and pleasure. The scale, together with standardization information and directions for administration and scoring, was issued in Terman's *Measurement of Intelligence* (1916), which immediately became the standard work on the subject.

The Stanford-Binet maintained its position of unquestioned prestige for more than two decades when it was revised by Terman and Maud Merrill (1937). A third revision was issued in 1960, soon after Terman's death. Terman's lifetime contributions did not add greatly to theory of measurement but were of great value for the application and usefulness of tests, and for the psychology of individual differences. In his autobiography, he wrote concerning his work:

> I think I saw more clearly than others the possibilities of mentality testing, have succeeded in devising tests that work better than their competitors, and by application of test methods, have added to the world's knowledge of exceptional children. (In Murchison, ed., 1932)

Although the 1916 Stanford-Binet retained the overemphasis on verbal skills characteristic of the earlier Simon-Binet series and contained no test for the eleven-year level, it was far superior in reliability and validity to its predecessors. Moreover, for the first time in the history of testing, a series of explicit, well-organized instructions was provided for administering and scoring the tests. Terman also made it clear that deviations from the standard procedure for administering the scale were likely to cause serious errors in the test results.

The basic measure employed to report performance on the scale was Stern's (1912) "mental quotient" concept, which Terman multiplied by 100 to eliminate the decimal point and renamed *intelligence quotient* or "I.Q." Because Stern did not incorporate this index as a basic feature of a mental test, the concept received little attention until Terman employed it in the 1916 Stanford-Binet. He presented the distribution of I.Q.'s obtained with the scale for the standardization sample and suggested a classification scheme for interpreting the IQ that is still quoted without change in many textbooks: IQ's from 90 to 110 indicate normal intelligence; an I.Q. below 70 indicates definite feeblemindedness; an I.Q. above 140 indicates genius. He took care to point out that the limits set in the table were defined arbitrarily and that the classification scheme itself was intended only as a general guide for the use of the new measure. Unfortunately, these cautions were soon disregarded by many persons dazzled by evidence of marked contrasts in school achievement and general behavior of children with high and low I.Q.'s. People, among whom were both educators and psychologists, came to view the I.Q. as an absolute, infallible index of mental capacity. Intelligence testing became a popular activity, and a favorite question was "what is your I.Q.?" At this same time, another important innovation in testing loomed on the horizon that was to add considerably to the popularity of this question.

Arthur Otis

A unique innovation in the mental measurement movement was introduced by Arthur Otis (1886–1964), one of Terman's graduate students. In 1912, Otis approached Terman with the idea of devising tests that would function as the individually administered Simon-Binet Scale did but which could be presented to many people at the same time. Terman supported this idea and encouraged Otis to proceed with his plans. For five years, Otis worked to develop a pool of items which could be administered to groups. From his pool of items, Otis arranged selected items into a formal scale which, in 1916 and 1917, first was standardized on a representative sample of the Stanford area population. This scale, a description of its development, and a discussion of its standardization were published in two issues of the *Journal of Educational Psychology* (Otis, 1918a and 1918b).

The Otis *Absolute Point Scale* was essentially a battery of tests containing two complete sets of items, each set including the same types of items but with different specific content. It would seem, therefore, that Otis introduced the concept of alternate forms for group tests of mental ability. The ideas for the types of items used were derived from various sources, but chiefly from Terman's Stanford-Binet. Basically accepting, as had Terman, the Binet model of intelligence and working in proximity to Terman and Terman's other students who were laboring on the revision of the Simon-Binet Scale, Otis adapted individually administered tasks for group testing and also developed new tasks. Otis' duplicate sets each contained items relevant to spelling, arithmetic, synonym-antonym, proverbs, disarranged sentences, relations, geometric figures, following directions, and narrative completion. Otis attributed the basic principle involved in his geometric items to A. R. Abelson. His narrative completion items involved the same content type as those used by Ebbinghaus, G. M. Whipple, Terman, and others. Synonym-antonyms, more than any other, were unique to the Otis scale (Yerkes, 1921). For all these tasks, Otis devised ingenious devices which permitted the responses of subjects to be given with a minimum of writing and which made possible objectivity in scoring. Although L. L. Thurstone at the Carnegie Institute of Technology had independently devised a stencil method of scoring an intelligence test at approximately the same time (1915) and Thorndike had used a stencil as early as 1914 to score his reading test, "Otis seems to have been the first to arrange a battery of intelligence tests so that they could be scored exclusively by stencils" (Yerkes, 1920a).

Although group testing as applied to other than school subjects had been employed by T. L. Bolton as early as 1892, in general, Otis has been regarded as the pioneer in group mental ability testing. This acknowledgement, however, has not gone uncontested. For example, T. L. Kelley (1927) cited Naomi Norsworthy as the author of the first battery of group tests of intelligence (1906), which was used in her research on mentally deficient children. On the other hand, W. S. Miller (a former student of G. M. Whipple at the University of Michigan) argued that he, not Otis, first generated the concept of group testing (Miller, 1922). Miller stated that the value of group testing was emphasized in his doctoral research, completed and published in 1914, thus antedating Otis' completed work by several years. He asserted that his thesis, *Mental tests and the performance of high-school students as conditioned by age, sex, and other factors*, was the basis for development of a set of test items that could be administered to groups of high-school students. However, the resulting instrument, the *Miller Mental Ability Test*, was not published until 1922, long after the parent Otis test had been issued and after the Otis style and format had been proven successful by the Army group tests. Miller's argument has fallen on deaf ears. Otis has continued to be recognized for his pioneer work in group ability testing.

Trial by Fire

The Otis contributions to group mental ability testing quickly faced the test: trial by a world at war. With the entry of the United States into World War I in April, 1917, several scientific problems of psychological nature were forced upon the attention of military authorities. Accordingly, the National Research Council organized the General Committee on Psychology for the purpose of organizing and supervising psychological research and service in the war effort. Robert M. Yerkes, a psychology professor at Harvard University and the then new president of the American Psychological Association, was appointed Chairman of this committee. James McKeen Cattell, G. Stanley Hall, and E. L. Thorndike represented the National Academy of Sciences; Raymond Dodge, S. I. Franz, and G. M. Whipple represented the American Psychological Association; and C. E. Seashore, J. B. Watson, and R. M. Yerkes (Chairman) represented the American Association for the Advancement of Science. Problems suggested by military officers or by psychologists were to be referred by the general committee to appropriate individuals or institutions for prompt attention.

Eleven sub-committees were organized by the General Committee on Psychology to deal with either psychological problems per se or problems involving a psychological aspect. The plans formulated by these committees were submitted to the War Department during the summer of 1917 and, with revision, subsequently were approved. Several significant lines of psychological services to the war effort evolved from these plans. Under the Adjutant General, the Committee on Classification of Personnel in the Army developed and introduced throughout the army methods of classifying and assigning enlisted men in accordance with occupational and educational qualifications and methods of rating officers for appointment and promotion.

> The services of this committee, to the work of which the War Department dedicated nearly a million dollars, ultimately touched, and more or less profoundly modified, almost every important aspect of military personnel work. (Yerkes, 1920)

Psychological service was rendered to the Signal Corps and, subsequently, to the Division of Military Aeronautics in connection with the selection and placement of men and the measurement of the effects of high altitude. The effective promotion of interest in measures for the control and improvement of both military and civilian morale ultimately resulted in the organization of a Morale Branch within the General Staff of the Army. Psychological methods were devised or adapted for the Division of Military Intelligence to assist in the selection, placement, and effective training of scouts and observers. Requests from the Chemical Warfare Service led to the study of psychological problems presented by the gas mask, and major recommendations resulting from these psychological investigations were embodied in the development of improved forms of the mask. Service to the Navy took the form of methods and mechanical devices for the proper selection, placement, and training of gunners, listeners, and lookouts.

A Division of Psychology was organized within the Medical Department of the Army for the administration of mental tests to enlisted men and commissioned officers in accordance with plans developed by the Committee on the Psychological Examining of Recruits. This Committee was chaired by R. M. Yerkes and included W. V. Bingham (Secretary), H. H. Goddard, T. H. Haines, L. M. Terman, F. L. Wells, and G. M. Whipple. Between May 28 and June 9, 1917, Yerkes' committee met at the Training School, Vineland, New Jersey, where Goddard was research director. Problems of particular importance that faced the committee were: (1) the identification of intellectually incompetent recruits; (2) the selection of men for special tasks; (3) the identification of the psychotic; and (4) the mental diagnosis of incorrigibles. The committee concluded that because intelligence tests offered the best possibilities of practical service, their work should be confined primarily ". . . to the classification of recruits on the basis of intellectual ability, with special reference to the elimination of the unfit and the identification of exceptionally superior ability" (Yerkes, 1921). Furthermore, it was agreed that an effort should be made to examine the mental ability of all recruits. Responsibility for the assessment of psychotics and other emotionally disturbed individuals was assumed subsequently by R. S. Woodworth and his Committee on Problems of Emotional Stability, Fear, and Self-Control.

The Committee on the Psychological Examining of Recruits immediately was confronted with the obvious conclusion that time-consuming individual methods of examining were inappropriate for the huge task at hand. Fortunately, with Arthur Otis' generous permission, Terman had brought to the meeting not only the Otis system of group tests but also the entire manuscript of Otis' *Absolute Point Scale*, together with the correlational data it had yielded. Moreover, several other members of the committee, namely Bingham, Wells, and Whipple, also had recent encouraging experiences with various types of group tests, while working with the Division of Applied Psychology (Bingham, Director) at the Carnegie Institute of Technology. The committee agreed that such group tasks as these, or others of similar nature, could be adapted readily for army needs.

Criteria for determining the value of a mental test were identified: (1) adaptability for group use; (2) validity as a measure of intelligence; (3) range of intelligence measured; (4) objectivity of scoring; (5) rapidity of scoring; (6) resistance to coaching; (7) inhibition of malingering; (8) inhibition of cheating; (9) independence of schooling; (10) limitation upon writing in responses; (11) interest and appeal; and (12) economy of time. Thirteen different tests were selected on the basis of their capability for more or less satisfactory adaptation to meet these requirements. Five members of the committee (Haines, Terman, Wells, Whipple, and Yerkes) rated all 13 tests on a scale of 1 to 5 for each of the 12 criteria listed. On the basis of a composite rating for each of the tests, ten tests were selected to compromise the group scale.

The resultant scale for group testing, *Group Examination A*, exhibited a close resemblance to the Otis scale. Of the ten subtests in *Group Examination A*, four ". . . were taken from the Otis Scale practically without change, and certain others were shaped in part by suggestions derived from the Otis series" (Yerkes, 1921). The contribution of the committee with respect to the original Army scale was chiefly in terms of adaptations designed to render the tests more serviceable for military use (Yerkes, 1921). Test 1, Oral Directions, adapted the best features of the Following Directions tests of R. S. Woodworth and F. L. Wells and of A. R. Abelson. It differed from Otis' Geometric Figures Test in that directions were given orally instead of being read by the subject. Test 2, Memory for Digits, was the Otis adaptation for group use of the Stanford-Binet Memory Span Test. Test 3, Disarranged Sentences, was the Otis adaptation of the Stanford-Binet Disarranged Sentences Test. Test 4, Arithmetic Reasoning, utilized no new concept and primarily involved the four fundamental mathematical processes and simple fractions. Test 5, Information, was borrowed in part from Wells' Information Test and in part from the *Bureau of Salesmanship Research Tests* devised by Bingham and Whipple. Test 6, Otis Synonym-Antonym, was taken intact from the Otis *Absolute Point Scale*. Test 7, Practical Judgment, was a cross between the Stanford-Binet Comprehension Test and F. G. Bonser's Selective Judgment Test. Test 8, Number Series Completion, was based upon the Number Series Completion Test of L. L. Thurstone. Test 9, Analogies, was an adaptation of Woodworth and Wells' Mixed Relations Test, using the Otis, Bingham, and Thurstone form. Test 10, Number Comparison, was proposed by Wells as an improved form of a cancellation test.

As a result of committee agreement that ten equivalent forms of each test should be prepared as a safeguard against coaching, the ten subtests were assigned to various members of the committee for the preparation of items for nine equivalent forms to match the original Army scale. Memory for Digits, Information, Number Series Completion, and Number Comparison were assigned to Wells; Analogies and Synonym-Antonym to Terman; Disarranged Sentences and Practical Judgment to Haines and Goddard; Oral Directions to Whipple; and Arithmetic Reasoning to Bingham. The method used to secure alternative forms of equal difficulty was the random selection technique proposed by Wells. It was decided that each test in the scale should contain from 10 to 40 items ranging from easy to difficult and that the time limit should not exceed three minutes per test. Moreover, the time allowed for each test should permit no more than five percent of an average group to attempt all of the items.

Having decided upon these group examination procedures, the committee then focused its attention upon the problem of devising methods for individual assessment. It was agreed that such methods would be necessary for further testing of men ranking low on the group scale, for those ranking in the highest five or ten percent, and for those whose scores were irregular or atypical. The committee believed that men who ranked low on the group scale would include not only genuinely subnormal persons but also foreigners and others handicapped by illiteracy. In view of these purposes, specific criteria were established for the individual tests, and some 50 tests were suggested by the committee from among already existing tests proven to be of value as measures of intelligence. These were subjected to critical evaluation and 21 tests (later increased to 22) were selected. These tests were not combined into a single scale, because only certain tests were to be used for the particular individual problem indicated by a given group scale score. Five alternative sets of items were prepared for all but six of these tests. After brief use in the Army, these individual tests generally were abandoned in favor of the Stanford-Binet and *A Point Scale for Measuring Intelligence* (Yerkes, Bridges, and Hardwick, 1915), chiefly because of the lack of norms for the interpretation of scores. Detection of illiteracy was attempted later by means of three literacy tests developed or adapted for group use, but these also proved unsatisfactory and eventually were replaced by a new group intelligence scale for foreign and illiterate subjects.

During the middle of June, Yerkes' committee adjourned for two weeks in order to try out the methods which had been devised. From June 10–23, approximately 400 examinations were made of U. S. Marines and candidates in officers' training camps. The measurements were analyzed by the committee and used as the basis for revision of the tests and for devising methods of scoring. Within the short span of six weeks (May 29 to July 7, 1917), the committee at Vineland had accomplished a truly amazing feat:

1. It had developed a plan for the psychological examination of an entire military force;
2. It had prepared an intelligence scale that permitted the examination of hundreds of men at a time by a single psychologist and was ". . . all but immune from the personal equation of the examiner and wholly free from the personal equation of the scorer" (Yerkes, 1921);
3. It had demonstrated the reliability and validity of the group scale by trial upon 400 subjects;
4. "It had made the scale reasonably 'coachproof' by preparing ten alternative forms which were entirely nonduplicated in matter but psychologically identical and of approximately equal difficulty" (Yerkes, 1921);
5. It had devised methods of individual examination to be used with subjects for whom the group examination might be inadequate or inconclusive;
6. It had prepared five alternative series of items for all but six of the individual tests in order to reduce the effects of coaching;
7. It had prepared copy for an *Examiner's Guide* which contained directions for the conduct of the examinations, and an edition of 5,000 copies of the revised group scale was in press to be used for further trial and experimentation;
8. It had formulated a plan for a thorough trial of the methods with military subjects.

Arrangements for an extensive trial of the examination methods were made by Bingham and Yerkes at various Army and Navy stations. Approximately 4,000 men were examined at the following locations: Fort Benjamin Harrison, Indianapolis, Indiana (Chief Examiner, G. M. Whipple); Camp Jackson, Nashville, Tennessee (Chief Examiner, E. K. Strong); Reorganization Camp, Syracuse, New York (Chief Examiner, J. W. Hayes); Naval Training Base No. 6, Brooklyn, New York (Chief Examiner, R. S. Woodworth); and several institutions for mental defectives. The results were sent to a statistical unit at Columbia University under the direction of Thorndike, assisted by Otis and Thurstone. A comparison of the group results with officers' ratings of the men tested yielded a correlation coefficient of approximately .50 and, in general, verified the belief that the new methods would be appropriate for military use. In accordance with recommendations made by Thorndike, the methods were modified and supplemented.

As a consequence of this official trial, a revised plan for the psychological examining of recruits was prepared and submitted through the

National Research Council to the Surgeon General of the Army, W. C. Gorgas. This plan proposed that six qualified psychological examiners be commissioned in the Army, each to be in charge of the work of a single camp, and that 18 assistant psychological examiners be appointed under the Civil Service Commission. Specific recommendations for equipment and for the method of procedure in examining also were included. Furthermore, it was recommended:

> . . . that all recruits, on the results of the group examination, be tentatively classified as mentally (a) low, (b) high, (c) average, (d) irregular; and that as time permits the lowest ten percent, the highest five percent, and irregular individuals shall be subjected to more searching individual examination. (Yerkes, 1921)

On August 17, 1917, work officially began with Yerkes' acceptance of an appointment as Major in the Sanitary Corps* to organize and direct psychological examining for the Medical Department of the Army. A plan for an official trial of these methods in four National Army cantonments was submitted to the Secretary of War, Newton D. Baker, together with the request for authorization of civil appointments for this work. Sixteen psychologists were commissioned and assigned in groups of four men each to Camp Lee (Virginia), Camp Taylor (Kentucky), Camp Dix (New Jersey), and Camp Devens (Massachusetts). By October 1, 1917, psychological testing was in progress in all four camps. Preliminary reports of the results were made available on October 20, and "*Group Examination A,* on which the success of the army examining chiefly depended, was found to be satisfactory in all except minor details" (Yerkes, 1921). The reactions of a sample of line officers ($N = 310$) relative to the value of psychological examinations generally were favorable (82% favorable, 18% unfavorable). However, these reports also revealed:

> . . . (1) surprisingly high frequency of illiteracy; (2) extreme differences in frequency of illiteracy and in distribution of intelligence for companies of a given regiment; (3) urgent need of a good group method of examining foreign and illiterate subjects. (Yerkes, 1921)

In November, a Section of Psychology was created within the Division of Neurology and Psychiatry, Office of the Surgeon General. Major Yerkes was placed in charge of the section which also included Captain S. Berry, Lieutenant A. S. Otis as statistician, and L. M. Ter-

---

* Yerkes and other psychologist officer personnel were commissioned first in the Sanitary Corps, because this was the only Army branch at that time under the command of the Surgeon General which did not require status as a licensed medical professional as a qualification for a commission.

man (later Major) as an advisory member. On January 19, 1918, upon the recommendation of the Surgeon General, the War Department granted approval of a plan for the extension of psychological examining to the entire Army, *with the exception of field and general officers.* Preparations were begun immediately for a thorough revision of all the initial examination methods. Furthermore, plans were made to establish a school of military psychology to train needed commissioned and enlisted personnel.

The Section of Psychology was reorganized as a Division of Psychology in the Office of the Surgeon General in January, 1918. A group of psychologists on military or civil appointment was assembled for the following specific purposes: (1) to revise *Group Examination A;* (2) to develop a substitute for the *Stenquist Group Test of Mechanical Skills* as a test for illiterates; and (3) to modify and supplement the methods of individual examination (generally abandoned in favor of the Stanford-Binet). Because of his close acquaintance with the conditions and results of examining in the Army camps, Captain C. S. Yoakum was charged with the responsibility of revising *Group Examination A* and was assisted by Lieutenant C. C. Brigham, Margaret V. Cobb, E. S. Jones, L. M. Terman, and G. M. Whipple. The development of a new group examination for illiterates was directed by Lieutenant W. S. Foster, who collaborated with C. R. Brown, A. S. Otis, K. T. Waugh, and R. H. Wheeler. As a result of using the Army mental tests in high schools and colleges, L. M. Terman and O. M. Haggerty supplied data that proved to be extremely valuable for the revision of examining methods. The purposes of securing these data were to make available age and grade norms for the Army tests and to measure the validity of tests for other than Army groups.

The revision of *Group Examination A*, called *Group Examination Alpha* to distinguish it from both the original scale and the new *Group Examination Beta* for foreign and illiterate subjects, was completed by April, 1918, and immediately was placed in use. Between April 1 and December 1, 1918, *Group Examination Alpha* was administered to approximately 1,250,000 men. The major change in the revised examination was the elimination of Test 2 (Memory for Digits) and Test 10 (Number Comparison), because both had a low correlation with Stanford-Binet mental age scores and other measures of intelligence. In general, major changes in the other eight tests of *Group Examination A* involved increasing the number of items, arranging the items to conform more closely with their order of difficulty, and eliminating items found to be too easy. Because the new *Beta* examination was expected to provide accurate ratings of men below a fourth-grade literacy level and of those obtaining grades below C in the

Alpha examination, the revision of *Group Examination A* ". . . was guided by the belief that the new scale should permit the strongest individuals to distinguish themselves from those of moderate ability" (Yerkes, 1921). Five alternate forms (Forms 1–5) of *Group Examination Alpha* were prepared. The total administration time for this scale was approximately 50 minutes.

The original form of *Group Examination Beta* consisted of 15 tests, most of which were essentially *Examination A* tests translated into pictorial form in order that pantomime and demonstration could be substituted for written and oral directions (Yerkes, 1920). The preliminary investigation of *Group Examination Beta* revealed that group intelligence tests for foreign and illiterate subjects were feasible and that the procedure employed was relatively satisfactory. However, the 15 tests were not found to be of equal validity or practicability. The total score of eight of the tests did correlate highly (.79) with *Group Examination Alpha* total score and produced ". . . a fairly sharp distinction between groups known to differ in intelligence" (Yerkes, 1921). The other seven tests added no appreciable increment to the validity of the scale.

The task of revising *Group Examination Beta* in accordance with the results of its preliminary trial was undertaken in February and March, 1918, by Major Yoakum with the help of Lieutenants Brigham and Otis and Miss Cobb. The choice of tests for the final scale was determined by the following considerations: (1) correlation with both *Alpha* and *Beta* total scores; (2) differentiation among average, low, and institutionalized subjects; (3) clarity of directions; (4) economy of time in administration and scoring; and (5) economy of space occupied in the record blank. The revised *Group Examination Beta*, made available for camp use in April, 1918, contained eight tests: Maze, Cube Analysis, X-O Series, Digit Symbol, Number Checking, Pictorial Completion, Geometrical Construction, and Spot Pattern. Subsequently, however, Spot Pattern (Test 8) was dropped from the scale on the basis of evidence that its inclusion added no appreciable increase in correlation between *Beta* total score and the Stanford-Binet.

The plan approved for the extension of psychological examining to the entire army ". . . explicitly included the provision of the necessary commissioned and enlisted personnel, the establishment of a school for military psychology, and the construction of a special building in each camp or cantonment" (Yerkes, 1921). The School of Military Psychology was organized at the Medical Officers' Training Camp (Camp Greenleaf), Fort Oglethorpe, Georgia, with a staff of seven psychologists headed by senior instructor, Captain W. S. Foster. Approximately 100 officers and more than 300 enlisted men received training between

February 4, 1918, and January 9, 1919, when the school was closed. The roster of the first company of commissioned psychologists to complete its training reads like a partial "Who's Who in American Psychology" of that decade.

With the steady flow of commissioned and enlisted personnel completing training at Camp Greenleaf, the work of the Division of Psychology was organized finally in 35 army training camps. Prior to January 1, 1919, psychological examinations were administered to a grand total of 1,726,000 men. Approximately 41,000 of this number were commissioned officers. Individual examination was made of more than 83,000 of the enlisted men in addition to the group examinations for literates, illiterates, or both.

Of the 1,566,011 men tested between April 28, 1918, and January 31, 1919, approximately 25.3 percent of them ". . . were unable to read and understand newspapers and write letters home" (Yerkes, 1921). *Group Examination Beta* was administered to these men and to an additional 5.7 percent who had failed *Group Examination Alpha*. It was estimated that more than one-half of this combined group were native-born Americans. The results of individual examination yielded evidence that 46,347 men possessed mental ages below ten years. Of this group, 7,800 men were recommended for discharge; 10,014 men were recommended for assignment to labor battalions; and 9,487 were recommended to development battalions for careful observation and preliminary training in order to discover, if possible, ways of using them successfully in the Army. Thus, approximately two percent of all men examined during this period were considered unfit for regular military service.

The original purpose of the army tests, i.e., to identify those recruits whose defective intelligence would make them a menace to the military organization, was achieved successfully. However, the military value of early and reliable estimates of the general intelligence of each recruit proved to be far greater than had been anticipated. This work was praised highly by Major General Hutchinson, Director of Organization of the British Army. In an address at the Personnel Officers' School in 1918, General Hutchinson contrasted British and American military personnel policies. He spoke quite frankly of the serious mistake Great Britain had made in recruiting skilled labor indiscriminately into fighting units: "They made good soldiers, but the plan seriously interfered with the development of technical units and the 'output of many vital things'" (Yoakum and Yerkes, 1920).

Major Yerkes, speaking before the Harvey Society (medical) of New York on January 25, 1919, suggested the future role the Army tests would have in civilian life:

. . . Before the war mental engineering was a dream; today it exists, and its development is amply assured. From leaders in our school systems, from administrative officers and leaders in colleges and professional schools, and from specialists in educational psychology come requests for permission to use the army mental tests. (Yerkes, 1920)

However, the successful applications to the American war effort of the results obtained from military testing were due in large measure to the strict limitation of their use to the intended purposes. Therefore, educational, industrial, or social applications of the army tests ". . . must necessarily be less successful in that degree (to) which the aim and the groups tested differ from the selected group reporting to the great cantonments to be trained as soldiers." (Yoakum and Yerkes, 1920) Nonetheless, the road was paved solidly for the future growth of mental measurement by its proven effectiveness during the war years. The tasks of formulating new standards for the Army tests and of developing new tests for school, industrial, and social purposes were assigned to the post-war decade of the 1920's.

3

....

Between Two Wars
and a Bit Beyond

The echos of the last cannon shot scarcely had died away when a host of requests deluged the Surgeon General's Office from both psychologists and school personnel seeking permission to use the Army tests. At the same time began an intensive campaign to develop new group tests of intelligence and of achievement. A third stage in the movement for the scientific measurement of intellectual processes and products appeared to have arrived. Much later, a British psychologist, J. O. Irwin, was to suggest that any new scientific technique seems to go through four stages:

> The first is the early stage of development when no one, except its inventors, is interested in it, and those working on other lines regard it with indifference or suspicion, or think it silly. In the second stage it begins to gain support, and in the third stage everyone wants to use it whether they understand it or not. There is then danger of a fourth stage of disillusionment, and this is the time for critical examination. (Irwin, 1934)

With respect to the standardized test movement in America, the first *stage of indifference, suspicion, and hostility,* with which Rice's spelling inquiry was met, largely had disappeared by the end of the first decade of the present century when the first standardized tests appeared. During the second decade came a *stage of curiosity,* when testing began to gain support. In this stage, tests were tried out ". . . merely because they were something new and because their use gave evidence, if indeed superficial in character, of up-to-date-ness" (Ross, 1947). Following World War I, a *stage of confidence* set in. Standardized tests were "swallowed hook, line, and sinker." Test results were accepted uncritically at their face value. I.Q.'s were regarded naively as accurate and absolute measures of innate capacity wholly apart from any consideration of an individual's environmental opportunities:

> As many of the subjects tested were children of school age, because Binet's scores gave a good correlation with ability for school work, and because of the relative simplicity and economy of the methods, mental testing was oversold, and careful psychological work in the field of individual differences still suffers from this effect. (Maxfield, 1936)

A parallel situation was effected in educational measurements. Achievement test results were accepted as completely adequate measures of the important outcomes of instruction. Provided that such instruments could be scored objectively, they were assumed to be sufficiently accurate for valid comparisons of not only one school or one class with another but also one pupil with another, and even of one aspect of a given pupil's achievement with another aspect of that same pupil's achievement. Walter S. Monroe (1935) accurately summarized the situation: "In the widespread use of objective tests . . . there is apparent a child-like faith in the efficacy of objective tests as instruments for measuring school achievement. . . . A little knowledge has become a dangerous thing." Although this comment characterized mental measurement in the early years after the Armistice, by no means was the period devoid of its "wanderers in the wilderness" who sought to promote critical caution in the use of tests and to provide, by continued experimentation, authoritative research findings that would result in improved measures and in intelligent interpretation of test data.

Post-War Boobus and Boom

Following the Armistice of November, 1918, the nation was shocked to learn that approximately three percent of young American men had mental ages below ten years. Moreover, the mental age of the average American soldier was found to be only 13.5 years. H. L. Mencken made the gloomy appraisal that ". . . a new breed of man was being spawned in the Western Hemisphere — 'Boobus Americanus' " (Reisman, 1966). In defense of the mentality of America's young men, Yoakum and Yerkes (1920) emphasized the fact that, because the Army tests sampled a limited range of abilities, a person might score low on them but yet be able to perform other skills in superior fashion. Moreover, F. N. Freeman (1926) pointed out that the procedure employed for determining the mental ages of the Army examinees assumed that scores made by children and by adults on the same mental test represented equivalent mental capacities. Conclusive evidence derived from the results of Army testing indicated to Freeman (1926) that such an assumption was not valid:

> While the discrepancy may be explained in part by other minor factors, the chief explanation must be this lack of equivalence of the results of the test given to children who are in school and are accustomed to doing tasks similar to those demanded by the tests, and to adults who have been out of school for from six to ten years or more, and have lost a good deal of their adeptness for performing tasks which involve clerical skills.

Challenged by Mencken's "Boobus Americanus" epithet, certain other psychologists also initiated investigations of the validity of this assertion. Terman (1919), using the Army group tests and his own Stanford-Binet, studied the intelligence of school children. Carl C. Brigham (1923) reported a broader survey of American intelligence. W. F. Book (1923) and C. W. Odell (1925) investigated the intelligence of high school students, while A. H. McPhail (1924) and Ben H. Wood (1923) studied college students.

As early as the 1920's, it was recognized by a few measurement experts that intelligence tests were subject to definite limitations: (1) they measure intellectual capacity indirectly rather than directly; (2) they are restricted to measuring only samples of behavior that are assumed to be representative of an individual's total behavior; and (3) the behaviors being measured are conditioned not only by native endowment but also by experience and training. These limitations of intelligence tests, applicable with slight modification to achievement tests also, remain as limitations of the most modern and carefully developed standardized tests of the 1960's. Even though these limitations were identified very early, this recognition merely served to heighten the ardor of psychologists for the development of tests that would be as valuable as were the Army tests during World War I.

Within five years after the cessation of hostilities in November, 1918, approximately fifty group tests of mental ability had been developed and published for use in American schools and colleges. In his presidential address before the APA in 1924, Terman emphasized the valuable contributions to the science of psychology that were being made and that could be made in the future by the use of mental tests. Tests were thought to be useful in solving particular problems such as those associated with the measurement of individual and race differences, the structure and inter-relationships of mental traits, the evaluation of intellectual growth, the limits of educability, and the understanding of genius, mental deficiency, and insanity.

Tests were becoming big business. Psychologists were delighted by the success of tests but objected to their commercialization. Adapted for all stages of intellectual development ranging from the kindergarten to college years, tests were employed not only in schools but also in clinical settings, in industry, and in courts of the nation. The prospect of measuring intelligence by means of a short, simple test captured the imagination of both school personnel and the general public. Terms used in describing mental abilities were incorporated into everyday popular language. More than 2,500,000 intelligence tests were sold by one publishing firm during the single academic year of 1922–1923 (Freeman, 1926). The measurement of mental ability had become a recognized and accepted institution in the daily lives of American people.

Further evidence of the increasing use of tests was provided by the establishment of organizations for the development, standardization, and distribution of measurement instruments. By the middle of this century, these functions had become an important part of the business of at least 25 organizations in this country; 75 others published one or more tests or other measuring devices (Buros, 1953). For example, James McKeen Cattell took the lead in founding The Psychological Corporation in 1921. He was joined in this enterprise by a group of psychologists, some two hundred in number, who purchased shares of stock in the corporation. They were encouraged by reports from the British Institute of Psychology which indicated that psychological principles could be applied in industrial settings to increase both industrial production and individual satisfaction. In 1920, Morris S. Viteles set up a clinic at the University of Pennsylvania to promote vocational and industrial guidance. The aim of vocational guidance, according to Viteles, was to supply scientific direction in the choice of occupations. To achieve this aim required analysis of the demands of the job upon the individual and of the individual's abilities, interests, education and experience, temperament, health, physical appearance, and socioeconomic condition (Reisman, 1966).

Alpha et al.

After the *Army Group Examination Alpha* was released in 1919 by the War Department for general use, eight different revisions of the Army Alpha were prepared by various psychologists between 1920 and 1941. A large number of research studies on intelligence were conducted during the years between the two world wars in which the Alpha tests and other group intelligence tests were employed extensively. Most of the other intelligence tests were based upon the Army Alpha, hence the Otis model.

The original Otis test, the *Absolute Point Scale,* was renamed the *Otis Group Intelligence Scale, Advanced Examination* when the first edition was published for school use by the World Book Company in 1918. Designed for use in grades 5–13, this Otis test rapidly gained widespread application. However, in the early 1920's it was displaced by other tests which did not require as much time as did the Otis scale (one hour) and which could be administered even more easily. Otis' own *Self-Administering Tests of Mental Ability, Intermediate Examination* (1922b) for grades 4–9 and *Higher Examination* (1922a, 1929) for grades 9–13, were among the tests that displaced the original Otis scale. These Otis tests, in various revisions, have been available ever since. In 1936, Otis added a new series known as the *Otis Quick-Scoring Mental Ability Tests* (1936–1954), which quickly became popular and largely replaced the self-administering series. Two tests of the *Quick-Scoring* series, *Beta* and *Gamma,* were merely revisions of the earlier 1922 series which primarily introduced a new scoring format. The *Alpha* test, designed for grades 1–4, was completely new.

In the same year as the publication of the original Otis test, S. L. and Luella W. Pressey published their *Group Point Scale for Measuring General Intelligence* (1918) designed for use in high schools. The Pressey test had rather wide application during the 1920's, particularly in its short form (1920) which was employed in surveys of Indiana secondary schools. Although not utilized very extensively in public schools, G. M. Whipple's *Group Tests for the Grammar Grades* were devised as a result of his interest in organizing classes for gifted children. In 1917, he had begun an elaborate study of the effectiveness of many of the various individual test tasks for the specific purpose of identifying and selecting children for a special class of gifted pupils. Upon completion of his study (1919a), Whipple organized those tasks that had demonstrated the greatest value into his series of group tests

(1919b). The importance of this work was that schools began to focus attention upon the need to provide appropriate experiences for high ability children as well as for those in need of remedial instruction.

As another direct outgrowth of the Army tests, the Haggerty *Intelligence Examination: Delta 1* and *Delta 2* appeared on the market in 1919. M. E. Haggerty had been engaged in psychological service in the Army, although not in psychological examining. Nevertheless, he was very cognizant of the development of the Army tests and utilized this information when he developed his Delta 1 scale in connection with the Virginia School Survey (1919b). This test, a non-language scale, closely resembled the Army Beta and was intended for children in the primary school grades. Delta 2 for the upper school grades was similar to the Army Alpha. A number of tests based upon the Haggerty-Army Beta non-language model were developed subsequently by other psychologists. Notable among these were the *Dearborn Group Tests of Intelligence, Series I* (grades 1–3) and *Series II* (grades 4–9), devised in 1920 by W. F. Dearborn. Special features of these tests included content designed to appeal to children's interests and a greater variety of test tasks. Although some of the tasks were derived directly from the Army Beta (or Delta 1), other tasks were invented by Dearborn and were unique to his test. The *Primary Mental Test* devised by Rudolf Pintner and Bess V. Cunningham in 1923 was similar to the Dearborn tests in terms of item content. The Pintner-Cunningham test contained seven subtests, each involving responses to pictorial materials, and was the first of the Pintner series of tests which eventually covered all the school grades.

Probably the most important of the immediate post-war tests was the *National Intelligence Test* (1920) devised by the National Research Committee consisting of M. E. Haggerty, L. M. Terman, E. L. Thorndike, G. M. Whipple, and R. M. Yerkes. A grant of $25,000 was made to this committee by the General Education Board in order to "conduct researches and to devise tests which should be more highly refined than was possible without such extensive investigation" (Freeman, 1926). Resembling the Army Alpha, two scales (Scale A and Scale B) and two parallel forms of each scale were developed for grades 3–8. Other parallel forms were devised later. A unique feature of the *National Intelligence Test,* one that distinguished it from others of its time, was the inclusion of a practice exercise preceding each test. Subsequently, nearly all newly developed tests employed the practice exercise technique. The *National Intelligence Test* was used extensively, perhaps because of the committee's prestige. However, a major factor favoring its use was its large normative sample of approximately 4,000 children for each grade or age covered by the test. Freeman

(1926) reported that evidence of the scale having higher validity or greater reliability than other similar tests had not been demonstrated. Nonetheless, within a year after its publication, over 575,000 copies of the test were sold, and an additional 800,000 copies were distributed during the 1922–1923 academic year.

Most of the tests developed immediately after the war were organized as a series of graded tests with all similar test tasks segregated from dissimilar tasks. In addition, separate directions were provided for each of the individual tests in a scale, and each test was timed separately. A different type of organization was employed by L. L. Thurstone in his intelligence test designed for high school seniors and college freshmen. Thurstone's *Psychological Examination for College Freshmen* (1919b) contained a variety of test tasks arranged in rotation or cycles, rather than as segregated tasks in separate tests. Easy examples of the various tasks were placed at the beginning of a series, followed by slightly harder examples, with the most difficult tasks placed at the end of the series. When a new variety of task was introduced, it was explained by an example. Moreover, brief directions were given for each item. Major advantages of this format were that an examiner could give the general directions for the test to everyone at the beginning of a testing session and that the entire scale was timed as a unit, rather than timed separately for each item type. Performance on the Thurstone test was expressed in terms of a single score.

The Army Alpha scale was rearranged in the Thurstone fashion and was called popularly the "Scrambled Alpha" (Bregman and Cattell, 1925). Otis also adopted this form of organization for his *Self-Administering Tests of Mental Ability* series. Yet another series of tests to utilize this format were the *Henmon-Nelson Tests of Mental Ability*, devised by V.A.C. Henmon and M. J. Nelson and first published by the Houghton Mifflin Company in 1931. The Henmon-Nelson tests were designed for three levels involving grades 3–12 and contained 90 items of various types for each level, arranged in order of increasing difficulty. Performance on the tests was reflected by a single global score that emphasized verbal ability. These tests were revised by T. A. Lamke and M. J. Nelson in 1955. A fourth level for the college grades was issued in 1961 by Nelson, Lamke, and P. C. Kelso.

Thurstone changed his plan of test organization when he developed a second *Psychological Examination for College Freshmen* for the Committee on Personnel Research of the National Research Council. Published as the *American Council on Education Psychological Examination for College Freshmen* (ACE), this new test contained six separately timed parts and yielded not only a total score but also a "linguistic," or verbal, score and a "quantitative," or number, score.

New forms of this test were prepared annually for many years (1925–1954) by Thurstone and his wife, Thelma Gwinn Thurstone. Moreover, extensive normative data were obtained on a nationwide scale that involved different types of colleges. A similar examination was prepared by the Thurstones in 1933 for high school students. This test, the *American Council on Education Psychological Examination for High School Students* was revised each year from 1933–1947, and was employed extensively with success. In 1947, the Educational Testing Service, established at Princeton, New Jersey, merged and coordinated the functions formerly performed by the Graduate Record Office, the College Entrance Board, and the Cooperative Test Service. The following year, the Cooperative Test Division of the Educational Testing Service assumed responsibility for the ACE tests. These tests were discontinued a few years later (after 1954) and their functions were assumed by the *School and College Ability Test* (SCAT) of the Cooperative Test Division.

Among the most widely applied early group tests designed to assess the mental ability of college entrance applicants, in addition to the Thurstone tests, were E. L. Thorndike's *Intelligence Examination* (1918), S. S. Colvin's *Brown University Psychological Examination* (1920), H. A. Toops' *Ohio State University Psychological Examination* (OSUPE, 1919–1958) and the *Scholastic Aptitude Tests* (SAT, 1926–to date) of the College Entrance Examination Board. Thorndike has been credited with being the first advocator for the use of mental ability tests as an aid in selecting students for admission into college. His test immediately became required of all students seeking admission to Columbia University, and many colleges and universities quickly adopted this procedure. The Thorndike test was unique in its length, for it required more than three hours of administration, while most other tests of this period could be given in an hour or less. It was also different in that it included not only the usual general intelligence tasks but also subject-matter material drawn from high school subject areas, including a rather difficult reading test. The purpose of including the high school content material was to prevent students who were bright but poorly prepared from making an unduly high grade. A final point of difference for the *Thorndike Intelligence Examination* was its emphasis upon quality of performance and endurance, as distinguished from speed and alertness. Quality of performance was measured by providing a liberal time allowance and arranging a series of steeply graded item difficulty steps. The sheer length of this examination tested the factor of endurance.

While most psychologists agreed that it was desirable to measure the characteristics of quality and endurance, they disagreed as to whether the additional gain made from the longer length of the test was enough to compensate for the greater expenditure of time and effort in giving, taking, and scoring the test. Nonetheless, school personnel attested to the popularity of this test by their purchase of many copies during the years following its publication. The Thorndike test, however, as well as the Brown University examination, did not stand up well under the test of time. Both generally were replaced because of the continuing and greater popularity of the ACE, SAT, and the OSUPE. Of these three instruments, the SAT resembles the Thorndike examination most closely in terms of both test content (verbal and quantitative) and emphasis upon quality of performance and endurance. The OSUPE contains only verbal material that was organized into three parts: same-opposites, word analogies, and reading comprehension. The use of exacting test-construction procedures has typified the revisions of all three of these tests.

The practice of testing applicants for admission to college was extended to include graduate and professional schools when the *Miller Analogies Test* (MAT) was published in 1926. First developed for the selection of graduate students at the University of Minnesota, later forms of the MAT were made available to other graduate schools. However, administration of the MAT is restricted to licensed centers where strict controls can be exercised over the test materials in order to prevent coaching and to protect the security of the test. One form of the MAT has been made available for testing high-echelon industrial personnel. The MAT is confined solely to a series of complex analogies whose content was drawn from a broad cross section of academic fields. Research on intelligence test item types conducted over the years since the 1920's has provided evidence that the analogy item is one of the best discriminators at the higher level of academic experience. A difficult test, the MAT serves to differentiate among students whose scores clustered at the upper limit of such measures as the OSUPE.

A later test, also designed to provide a sufficient ceiling for superior individuals, was L. M. Terman's *Concept Mastery Test* (1956), which originated as a byproduct of his extensive longitudinal study of gifted children. The first form of this test, Form A, was developed for testing the intelligence of Terman's gifted group in early maturity (Terman and Oden, 1947). Form T was prepared for a later follow-up when the gifted subjects were in their mid-forties (Terman and Oden, 1959). Subsequently, Form T was released for more general use. The *Concept Mastery Test* includes both analogies and synonym-antonym items that are predominantly verbal in nature, although some numerical content is incorporated in the analogies items.

Most of the other tests designed for testing applicants seeking admission to college, graduate, and professional schools represented a combination of general intelligence and achievement tests. The *Graduate Record Examinations* (GRE) were originated in 1936 as a joint project of the Carnegie Foundation for the Advancement of Teaching and the graduate schools of four eastern universities. The GRE project was transferred to the Educational Testing Service in 1948. One part of the GRE, the Aptitude Test, is essentially a measure of general mental ability suitable for superior adults and yields separate verbal and quantitative scores. A second section of the GRE consists of Area Tests in Social Science, Humanities, and Natural Science. These tests represent a general achievement battery for the college level. Another set of achievement tests, the Advanced Tests, have been developed for many fields of specialization. The GRE were intended to measure breadth of cultural background, verbal comprehension, quantitative reasoning, and other qualifications considered important in the selection of graduate students. Similar tests or batteries of tests have been developed for the selection of applicants to professional schools such as schools of law, medicine, and dentistry.

Many other group tests of intelligence were developed and published during the years following the Armistice. The test of the 1920's rated by psychological experts to be the most reliable and valid was the *Terman Group Test of Mental Ability* (1920), designed for grades 7–12. The Terman test contained 370 well-constructed items in each of two forms and was purported to differentiate well between bright and dull pupils. Originally a total of 886 items had been tried out on a standardization sample, and only those items that could demonstrate reliability and validity of measurement were retained. Item content measured both verbal and quantitative thinking. The procedures for administering and scoring the test were simple, and the total time required for testing was 30–35 minutes. For the next 25 years, this test was one of the standard instruments for testing mental ability at the junior and senior high school levels. It was revised completely in 1942 by Terman in collaboration with Quinn McNemar. This revision, known as the *Terman-McNemar Test of Mental Ability*, undertook to incorporate the advances that had been made in both the theory and the mechanics of mental measurement between 1920 and 1940.

Late in the 1920's there appeared yet another series of tests that were destined to be widely used, the *Kuhlmann-Anderson Tests of Intelligence*. Preparation of the first edition (1927) of these tests was begun as early as 1916 by Frederick Kuhlmann for the purpose of conserving for group use as many of the desirable features of an individual test (the Simon-Binet) as was possible. In 1920, Rose G. Anderson joined Kuhlmann in his task of developing a group test. Dr. Anderson became responsible both for organizing the instructions for the tests and for the testing involved in the preliminary trials for the first edition and six subsequent revisions. Norms based upon the scores of several thousand children were presented for each test in terms of mental age corresponding to each point of score obtained.

Although they provided for converting mental age scores into intelligence quotients, these authors were strongly critical of this method. They preferred the *personal constant* method suggested by Heinis of Geneva, Swtizerland, as a substitute for the I. Q. The Heinis method utilized mental age expressed as percentage of average development (PA), and the results yielded a scale of Heinis Mental Growth Units. Except for the use made by Kuhlmann and Anderson, the Heinis PA method did not receive wide acceptance. It was omitted finally from the seventh and latest revised edition, the *Kuhlmann-Anderson Measure of Academic Potential* (1963), in favor of the widely accepted current emphasis on deviation score method or "deviation I.Q."

Relatively less dependent upon reading skill than most other group tests, the original edition of the Kuhlmann-Anderson tests contained 39 separately timed tests, each containing from 6 to 72 items, to be used in batteries of 10 tests appropriate for the age or grade of the person tested. Booklets containing the 10 tests suitable to a given grade were provided, and each battery required approximately 45 minutes for administration. When used for individual examination rather than group examination, the authors recommended that 14 tests constitute a battery, and separate test booklets were made available for this purpose.

As an outgrowth of a comprehensive research program on the measurement of intelligence by Thorndike and his colleagues (1927) at the Institute of Educational Research (IER) at Teachers College, Columbia University, an entirely different type of intelligence test was developed: the *I.E.R. Intelligence Scale,* or CAVD. The popular title was derived from the four parts of the test: Completion, Arithmetic, Vocabulary, and Directions. The test was highly verbal in content, for even the arithmetic problems frequently demanded a high level of reading comprehension. Although the CAVD scale was designed to assess mental abilities of a mental-age range of three years to superior adult, ". . . its best use appeared to be at the upper levels of intelligence, particularly where a non-time power test was desired" (Horrocks, 1964). Four new forms of the scale were prepared in 1935 for use on the college and higher levels. The CAVD scale yielded three different scores: (1) level of achievement, measured by determining at what level an individual was successful in answering one half of the items; (2) breadth of a particular level, determined by identifying the percent of items an individual passed at a given level; and (3) area of achievement, determined by summing the number of successes at all levels.

The CAVD scale represented the beginning of an important development in the mental measurement movement: a group intelligence measure which yielded results that could be reported in the form of several different psychologically meaningful categories. Providing several scores, the tests enabled the examiner to draw a profile of an examinee's performance in order to study a visual representation of his relative strengths and weaknesses. The CAVD scale, while purporting to be a test of several specific abilities, was interpreted as if it measured several outcomes of school instruction. Another example of the trend toward tests capable of yielding a graphic profile of an individual's multiple scores was the *California Test of Mental Maturity* (CTMM). The CTMM (1936–1963) was based upon Elizabeth T. Sullivan's rational analysis of the operations involved in the Stanford-Binet scale (1926) and has undergone periodic revisions since its initial publication.

Representative of the newer group intelligence tests in common use today are the *Lorge-Thorndike Intelligence Tests* (LTIT, 1954–1964) developed for the purpose of providing a continuous set of group tests measuring abstract reasoning ability for all school grades. Organized into verbal and nonverbal batteries, the LTIT deal with symbolic relationships which require the examinee to discover a principle and then apply it. These tests were designed, constructed, and standardized with exceptional care. A much needed innovation was supplied by the concurrent (1964) norming of the LTIT, the *Iowa Tests of Basic Skills*, and the *Tests of Academic Progress* in the same school systems at the appropriate grade levels in order to provide comparable intelligence and achievement scores for grades 3–12. The most recent of the tests that followed the trend established by Thorndike's CAVD scale are the *Academic Promise Tests* (APT), developed by G. K. Bennett and his co-workers (1961–1962) for the purpose of providing a broad and differential description of the abilities of students in grades 6–9. In many respects, these tests may be considered as a downward extension of these authors' *College Qualification Tests* (1958–1961) designed for grades 11–13. Moreover, there is strong resemblance between the four tests of the APT (Verbal, Numerical, Abstract Reasoning, and Language Usage) and the corresponding tests of the *Differential Aptitude Tests* (1947–1963) of the same author group for grades 8–12 and adults.

Beginning with the assessment of adults in the Army, group tests of mental ability quickly were extended downward to include, in order, the college and high school, junior high school, elementary, and finally the primary grades. During the early 1920's, interest in assessing the readiness of children for kindergarten and first grade work was expressed in the efforts of L. W. Cole and Leona E. Vincent that led to the development of the *Cole-Vincent Group Intelligence Tests for School Entrants* (1924). Standardized on a sample of 1171 pupils for whom Stanford-Binet mental ages were known, the Cole-Vincent tests were purported to measure (1) a child's understanding of language and his ability to follow verbal directions, (2) his ability to perceive form with special reference to likenesses and differences, and (3) his ability to translate with his hand what he saw with his eye. These authors recommended a promotion policy based on the findings of the test, a plan that arranged for pupils with high ability to complete three grades in two years by means of mid-year promotions. Although widely used by school systems for many years, both the tests and the recommended promotion policy generally were abandoned when detailed scientific work in the field of developmental readiness demonstrated that the test norms were of questionable value.

Functionally similar to the Cole-Vincent tests, the *Metropolitan Readiness Tests* (MRT, 1933–1965), designed for kindergarten and first grade entrants, tended to replace their predecessor and have continued to be the most widely employed of the school readiness tests. Developed by Gertrude H. Hildreth and Nellie L. Griffiths, these tests were intended to measure readiness for reading, arithmetic, and writing. The MRT norms indicated a significant relationship between scores on the test and first grade achievement. Moreover, evidence of the existence of high correlations between scores on the MRT and scores on intelligence tests was derived from numerous studies over the years. These correlations were approximately of the same magnitude as those that have been obtained between scores on different intelligence tests. Thus, it appeared that this readiness test served essentially the same purpose as an intelligence test. School personnel have varied in their preference for using first the one and then the other type of test, although the modern trend probably favors the use of a readiness test, supplemented when necessary by an individual intelligence test, for making decisions concerning school entrants into kindergarten and first grade.

The Binet Breed

Terman's *Stanford Revision of the Simon-Binet Scale* retained its popularity during the 1920's. However, there was a degree of dissatisfaction with this test, and other tests like it, and an awareness that much more needed to be done. Three problems were immediately recognized: (1) the lack of a suitable individually administered scale of intelligence for adults; (2) clarification of the concepts underlying tests in general and that of intelligence *per se;* and (3) the need for a suitable individually administered scale of intelligence for infants and young children. At first, virtually nothing was accomplished in producing an adult scale because of the controversy over the structure of intelligence that waxed and waned over the years. The need for an infant scale, however, was immediately urgent, particularly for use in adoption agencies and child-care institutions.

One of the earliest attempts to develop a standardized test for infants was Kuhlmann's 1922 revision of the Simon-Binet scales which extended these scales down to a three-month level. However, the pioneer work of Arnold Gesell and his co-workers at the Yale University Clinic of Child Development perhaps was more practicable and led to the publication of the *Gesell Developmental Schedules* (1925–1949) for children from four weeks through five years of age. The first of this series, the *Pre-school Child Test* (1925b) was accompanied by a manual entitled *The Mental Growth of the Preschool Child* (1925a), which presented Gesell's outline of normal child development from birth to the sixth year and included his system of developmental diagnosis. A revision of the initial test was released in 1938 as the *Gesell Maturity Scale.* Information about the tests, their revisions, and their standardization was issued in three separate publications: *The Psychology of Early Growth* (Gesell and Thompson, 1938); *The First Five Years of Life* (Gesell, *et al.,* 1940); and *Developmental Diagnosis* (Gesell and Amatruda, 1941). Of the three, *Developmental Diagnosis* was probably the most practical to use as a testing manual, because the record forms developed in this book were less complicated than those in the other books. Moreover, the directions were organized better for exploring the behavior of a given child in a testing situation. In general, the 1940 series of tests, the *Gesell Developmental Schedules,* represented a standardized procedure for observing and evaluating the course of behavior development in a child.

In their early form (1925a), the Gesell procedures, scoring, and standardization were described rather incompletely. Efforts to use the scale resulted in a variety of independently standardized adaptations, with each author interpreting them differently and establishing his own specific methods of administering and scoring essentially the same materials and testing situations. Some order was brought into this situation in 1940 when Psyche Cattell, the daughter of James McKeen Cattell, issued her *Infant Intelligence Scale* for ages 3–30 months. Developed as a downward extension of the 1937 Stanford-Binet, Form L, the Cattell scale was considered by many psychologists as one of the most satisfactory instruments for infant testing. In addition to Stanford-Binet items, the scale contained tasks from the *Gesell Developmental Schedules* and other available infant tests, together with some original items.

Among the tests designed especially for the preschool level were the *Merrill-Palmer Scale of Mental Tests* (Stutsman, 1931) for ages 24–63 months and the *Minnesota Preschool Scales* (Goodenough, Maurer, and Van Wagenen, 1932–1940) for ages 18 months to 6 years. The 38 tests in the Merrill-Palmer scale were selected from a total of 78 tests on the bases of popularity with children, practicality in administration, relation with ages, and differentiation of children judged by the Merrill-Palmer School staff to be bright or dull. These selected tests were administered then to a normative sample of 631 children (300 boys and 331 girls) between the ages of 18 and 77 months in Detroit, Michigan. The children were obtained from 20 different sources, including both public and private schools, orphanages, day nurseries, child-care agencies, health clinics, and the Merrill-Palmer waiting list. The scale's primary emphasis is upon motor skills and speed, with relatively few language tasks included. The principal asset of this scale has been its strong appeal to young children, both for the intrinsic interest of the tasks and for the manner of presenting the tests in attractive, gaily colored boxes. From the standpoint of preschool testing, an additional advantage stems from the scoring adjustments available for handling refusals and omissions. This test has played an important role in assessing abilities not tested by Binet-type scales.

The *Minnesota Preschool Scale* was derived largely from Kuhlmann's Binet scale (1922), with a few tasks taken from other individual scales and several original tasks added. Two equivalent forms were devised, each consisting of 26 tests. In contrast to the heavy motor skills emphasis of the Merrill-Palmer scale, the Minnesota scale contains relatively few motor tasks. The scale was classified into verbal and non-verbal types of tasks, each type yielding a separate score. The standardization sample, consisting of a carefully selected group of 900 children (including 100 at each half-year point from 1½ to 6 years of age), was obtained from nursery schools, public and private schools, settlement houses, and clinics. The sample was selected in terms of father's occupation in order to constitute a representative sampling of the population of Minneapolis. The major strengths of the *Minnesota Preschool Scale* appear to be the careful procedures followed in its standardization and in the development of its norms, the availability of parallel forms with their high parallel-form reliability, the elimination of speed, the reduction in number of motor skill items, and the extensive follow-up data (Anastasi, 1961). On the other hand, the tests in the scale proved to be not as appealing to young children (especially those under the age of three) as other preschool tests. Furthermore, the lack of any provision for handling refusals and omissions has been a handicap in testing preschool children. In this context, the practice of beginning with the easiest items in the scale, regardless of a child's age, tends to make the scale unduly long and boring for older and brighter children.

In 1928, Grace Arthur first released her *Point Scale of Performance Tests,* intended primarily for use with children between the ages of five or six to sixteen years. The purpose of the individually administered Arthur tests was to supplement, or to replace, the Binet rating on a child by administering a set of nonverbal tests, called "performance tests," because a child's abilities could not always be assessed adequately by a test that relied so heavily upon verbal responses alone, as did the Binet revisions. The various Binet revisions were entirely unsuitable for subjects who had a specific disability or handicap in the verbal area (e.g., deaf children), for those who spoke a language other than English, and for those with severe speech defects, as in cerebral palsy. Form I of this scale consisted of eight restandardized tests from the Pintner-Patterson *Scale of Performance Tests* (1917), together with the Kohs *Block-Design Tests* (1923) and the Porteus *Maze Test* (1924). A Revised Form II of the Arthur Performance Scale was released in 1947, as an alternate for Form I, for use in retesting. This form consists of five tests, one of which was the all-new Arthur Stencil Design Test. This subtest is somewhat similar to the Kohs *Block-Design test.* The other four tests are revised versions of the Knox *Cube test,* Seguin *Form-Board,* Porteus *Maze Test* and Healy *Picture Completion Test* that were included in the first form. The Arthur Performance Scale has been used widely as a nonverbal substitute, or supplement, for the Stanford-Binet revisions.

The Stanford-Binet was published in revised form in 1937 by Terman and Maude Merrill. Tests were provided at age levels from two years to a Superior Adult III category, including items for those levels which had been absent from the 1916 revision (11 and 13 years). There were two equivalent forms of the scale, L and M (the letters presumably referring to the first initials of its authors). The revision was standardized on a sample of about 3,000 American-born children ranging in age from one and a half years to eighteen years, and efforts were made to control the influence of geographic location and socioeconomic status.

Criticisms of the 1937 Revision of the Stanford-Binet were similar to those that had been made of the 1916 edition: there were too many verbal items; the test was of questionable value for adults; the use of mental ages at the upper end of the scale was misleading; it contained a hodgepodge of test items. Nevertheless, it was agreed generally that the 1937 Revision was a marked improvement over its predecessor. On the other hand, it was not such an improvement that the *Wechsler-Bellevue Intelligence Scale,* developed by David Wechsler and first published in 1939, was not welcomed as a new test having promise as an instrument for assessing the intellectual functioning of adults (Reisman, 1966).

David Wechsler (b. 1896) received his Ph.D. from Columbia University in 1925. At first his published interests centered upon evaluating the significance of the psychogalvanic reflex, but later he turned to the problems of measuring intelligence. In 1932, Wechsler accepted a position as Chief Psychologist at Bellevue Psychiatric Hospital in New York where he developed his test. The *Wechsler-Bellevue Intelligence Scale* was standardized upon 670 white children (from 7 to 16 years of age) and 1,081 white adults (ages ranging from 17 to 70 years), all of whom resided in New York City and surrounding areas. The scale was intended for use with persons from 10 to 70 years of age. Two forms were provided. Efforts were made to control for representativeness in terms of education and occupation.

Wechsler advocated the construction of intelligence scales in which there are relatively high intercorrelations among an extensive variety of subtests. Therefore, such scales could contain a relatively high saturation of Spearman's g. The resulting instrument was composed of Verbal and Performance Scales with five subtests in each scale: information, comprehension, arithmetic, similarities, and memory span for digits in the Verbal Scale; and object assembly, picture arrangement, block design, digit symbol, and picture completion in the Performance Scale. A vocabulary test was added as an alternate subtest. Wechsler rejected the mental age concept in favor of point scales. He assigned an IQ value of 100 to the mean score of an age group and an IQ value of 90 to a score that is minus one probable error from the mean. Thus, he was able to estimate IQ values for the conversion of raw scores for a particular age group on both the Verbal and Performance scales and on the Full Scale. In the case of adults, the scores obtained by an individual are compared with the scores of others of approximately the same age. In contrast, an adult's score on the Stanford-Binet is evaluated only in relation to the successes obtained by children and adolescents (Reisman, 1966).

In his development of the Wechsler-Bellevue, Wechsler found that, depending upon which specific subtest was involved, scores on his subtests decreased gradually for the ages between 15 and 22 years, and fell more rapidly after age 35. Wechsler's findings indicated to some psychologists that intellectual abilities continue to develop until early adulthood and then decline. To other psychologists, however, Wechsler's results continued to illustrate that intellectual growth varies with specific ability and with the means by which it is measured.

Publication of the Wechsler-Bellevue was timed propitiously, because World War II created a great demand for the evaluation of adult intelligence. In 1940, psychologists once again were called upon to develop tests for the evaluation of military personnel. A committee of psychologists consisting of Walter Bingham (Chairman), C. C. Brigham, H. E. Garrett, L. J. O'Rourke, M. W. Richardson, C. L. Shartle, and L. L. Thurstone formed an advisory group to the Adjutant General. These psychologists assisted in the development of the *Army General Classification Test* (AGCT), a group test administered to approximately ten million servicemen during the course of the war. When this test was replaced by a revised edition in 1945, the earlier form was released for civilian use (1947). A number of other tests, both individually and group administered, were devised for use in the selection of naval officers, pilots, instructors, and candidates for assignment to training in particular skills. Almost no American male adult of military potentiality escaped psychological testing during the war years. During this time, the Wechsler-Bellevue rapidly assumed the position of the leading individually administered adult intelligence scale.

As early as 1941, interest in the Wechsler-Bellevue was stimulated among clinical psychologists when Wechsler hypothesized that certain patterns of subtest score configurations might be useful in the diagnosis of organic brain disease, schizophrenia, mental deficiency, juvenile delinquency, and psychoneurosis (Reisman, 1966). Almost immediately, a flurry of research was produced to assess the instrument's validity as a diagnostic tool. An early evaluation of these studies published by Rabin (1945) indicated that the various Wechsler-Bellevue patternings might differentiate between groups of individuals who manifested certain psychiatric disturbances, but they were not sensitive enough to warrant a diagnosis in a specific case based upon this evidence alone.

In 1949, a similarly constructed *Wechsler Intelligence Scale for Children* (WISC) was published. A downward extension of the Wechsler-Bellevue, the WISC was standardized upon 100 boys and 100 girls at each of the 11 age levels from five through fifteen years. Consisting of white children only, this standardization sample was selected on the basis of age, presence or absence of feeblemindedness, urban and rural residence, occupational classification of fathers, and geographic location in the United States. The WISC has challenged the Stanford-Binet as the most popular individually administered intelligence scale for children, particularly with age ranges above eight years. Recently (1967) Wechsler has published a downward extension of the WISC, the *Wechsler Preschool and Primary Scale of Intelligence* (WPPSI). Constructed for ages four to six and one-half, the WPPSI was designed to provide the same types of measures as does the WISC. At present, few data are available to cast light upon the utility of this new test.

Only one individually administered scale published since 1950 has attained wide popularity: the 1955 *Wechsler Adult Intelligence Scale* (WAIS). The WAIS was normed on a population of 1700 persons of both sexes distributed over seven age levels between 16 and 64 years. Supplementary norms for older persons were established by testing an "old-age" sample of 475 persons 60 or more years old. The standardization sample was stratified carefully with proportionate representation in terms of education, occupational level, geographic location, race (white versus non-white), and urban versus rural populations within the United States. Ten percent of this sample was non-white. Despite the discouraging reports concerning the validity of pattern analysis when the original Wechsler-Bellevue was used for differential diagnostic purposes, Wechsler still included patterns of WAIS subtest scores for differentiating anxiety states, organic brain disease, delinquency, schizophrenia, and mental deficiency.

In all of his test construction work, Wechsler has remained loyal to Spearman's theory of the structure of intelligence. In so doing, Wechsler's position has been congruent with that professed by the majority of psychologists who have worked in the area of intelligence test construction. This is not to say that this point of view has not had its antagonists. The dialogue begun by Spearman and Thorndike prior to World War I was continued into the years that followed the "great war."

Another Armistice in the Air

It was a polite dialogue about the concept of intelligence that continued among psychologists. T. L. Kelley (1928) believed that there were three independent types, or factors, of intelligence: verbal, mathematical, and spatial (as evidenced in performance on such materials as form boards). In view of their independence, Kelley argued against the practice of adding up the scores of all the items on a scale to produce one total score. Thorndike also believed that there were three kinds of intelligence: a person's ability to deal with symbols, with people, and with objects. Spearman, of course, held to his view of a general factor of intelligence, *g*.

By 1927, Spearman had identified no less than four general factors in intelligence: g, the ability to educe relations and correlates; c, the degree of inertia in shifting from one task to another; w, the degree of determination or persistence evidenced in pursuing a task; and *oscillation*, the ease with which a person recuperates after expending effort. Both Spearman and Thorndike agreed that when a number of variables are correlated, these variables always can be factored into either a general factor and specific factors, or into a number of independent factors. By this date, the two systems of Spearman and Thorndike were seen to be interchangeable.

On the sidelines, however, it was advocated that the concept of intelligence be eliminated from psychology. Some psychologists believed that the IQ could be viewed merely as an index of certain types of adaptation. They argued that because intelligence scales sample heavily what a person has learned, they should be regarded as a form of achievement test. Therefore, all that the testing of intelligence did was simply to sample what the person had achieved as a basis for predicting what he would achieve. Thorndike interpreted the situation well:

> Existing instruments represent enormous improvements over what was available twenty years ago, but three fundamental defects remain. Just what measure is not known, how far it is proper to add, subtract, multiply, and divide, and compute ratios with the measure obtained is not known; just what the measures obtained signify concerning intellect is not known. (Thorndike, 1927)

From another point of view, Guy Fernald (1920), a physician, argued that intelligence and personality are blended. He considered it reasonable to think that culture can affect intellectual functioning by emphasizing or minimizing the development of certain skills. Similarly, William Stern (1925) cautioned against believing that the IQ represents only the individual's level of mental alertness and not his personality. An IQ makes possible the prediction of what a person cannot do but is less significant in making predictions about what a person will do. The impression that intelligence and personality are not distinct and separate functions was shared by persons other than these. By the late 1920's, not a few psychologists came to view three of the four general factors in intelligence described by Spearman as personality characteristics. Today, clinical psychologists are in agreement that nonintellective personality characteristics affect intellectual functioning. Much of their interest at this time centers on evaluating the effects upon intelligent behavior of various psychiatric disturbances, levels of anxiety, and a felt need for achievement. In general, research findings have indicated that there are optimum levels of anxiety and of need for achievement. Furthermore, there is general agreement that intellectual functioning is a complex process which is dependent upon satisfactory interpersonal relationships for normal development (Reisman, 1966).

As early as 1930, "the flaming controversy about the structure of intelligence had dwindled to a flicker, and most psychologists were content to sit back and let it burn itself out" (Reisman, 1966). However, L. L. Thurstone was not satisfied with this state of affairs. Soon another assault was launched against Spearman's position. The truce was over and the battle was resumed.

Factors Marching Up and Down Again

Born in Chicago of Swedish parentage, Louis Leon Thurstone (1887–1955) was educated in various elementary schools scattered around the eastern half of the United States and in Sweden. Graduating from high school in Jamestown, New York, Thurstone studied electrical engineering at Cornell University, where he became interested in the possibility of studying the learning function as a scientific problem. In his freshman year, he worked out an equation for a French curve to be used with a straight edge for trisecting any angle. This work resulted in his second publication. Thurstone's first publication was a short letter to the *Scientific American,* published in June, 1905, when he was in high school. Following graduation from Cornell, he demonstrated a model of a motion-picture projector to Thomas Edison, who promptly offered Thurstone an assistantship. Thurstone accepted the position and spent the next seven years working in Edison's laboratory.

Returning to academic life in the fall of 1912, Thurstone worked as an instructor in descriptive geometry and drafting at the University of Minnesota. During the next two years while teaching in the engineering college, he spent a great deal of time with Thorndike's former student, Robert Woodrow, who assisted Thurstone in an experimental study of the learning function. Completing a Master's degree in Engineering at the University of Minnesota in June, 1914, Thurstone began graduate study in Psychology under Professor J. R. Angell at the University of Chicago. Not overly impressed at first by either his fellow graduate students or some of his early courses in Psychology, Thurstone described these impressions in his autobiography:

> When they (graduate students in psychology) were asked a question, they would start to talk fluently, even when they obviously knew nothing about the subject. I was sure that engineers had higher standards of intellectual honesty. One of my first courses was called advanced educational psychology and it was taught by Professor Judd.

I used to wonder what the elementary course could be like if this was called advanced. I never had an elementary course in psychology or in statistics. (In Boring, Yerkes, and Werner, 1952)

In 1915, Walter Bingham offered Thurstone a graduate assistantship in the newly established Division of Applied Psychology at Carnegie Institute of Technology in Pittsburgh. Accepting the offer, Thurstone remained at Carnegie for the next nine years, first as a graduate assistant for two years and then on the staff as an instructor in statistics after obtaining his Ph.D. from the University of Chicago in 1917. His dissertation (published in 1919) concerned the learning curve equation and was the pioneer investigation of curve fitting in educational psychology. Both as a student and as a staff member at Carnegie, Thurstone became closely associated with Bingham and other well-known psychologists, most of whom were involved in the contributions that psychology made to the nation during World War I. (Among the psychologists at Carnegie at that time were Clarence Yoakum, G. M. Whipple, E. K. Strong, Jr., Kate Gordon, Walter Dill Scott, W. W. Charters, and J. B. Miner.) Thurstone's primary contribution to the war testing programs was his design of the key-word principle in oral tests.

The research activities of Carnegie's Applied Psychology Department flourished for eight years but were discontinued in 1923 when the Department lost favor with the Institute's administration. The following year, Thurstone married psychologist Thelma Gwinn, who also became his professional partner in their studies on psychological measurement, especially in the theoretical and experimental work on primary mental abilities. In 1924, the Thurstones returned to the University of Chicago where Thurstone had accepted an appointment as Associate Professor of Psychology. Thurstone also accepted a part-time appointment on the staff of Dr. Herman Adler at the Institute for Juvenile Research. This acceptance was a reflection of Thurstone's interest in the study of personality to which he returned several times during his career.

Although he introduced statistics into the psychology curriculum at the University of Chicago and continued to teach statistics courses, Thurstone turned his major attention to the teaching of mental test theory. Because there was no textbook suitable for his mental test theory classes, Thurstone prepared a lithoprinted monograph on the reliability and validity of tests entitled *Theory of Mental Tests* (1925). In 1926, Thurstone attacked and mildly damaged the concept of mental age by demonstrating its illogicality when applied to adults. At the root of the difficulty was the fact that scores on a particular test did not continue to increase with increasing age. Therefore, if mental age were defined as the average chronological age of people who made a certain test score, the mental ages for older children would be grossly inflated. This problem could be resolved easily, Thurstone suggested, by using as the test score an individual's percentile ranking with reference to his age group. Thurstone's suggestion had merit, but other psychologists believed teachers understood mental ages and would be confused by the percentile range method. Because of this attitude, little was done to implement Thurstone's suggestion.

Thurstone's theoretical and experimental work in multiple-factor analysis was initiated in 1929, although he had derived his original equation (1919a) when he was still at Carnegie. Although T. L. Kelley's *Crossroads in the Mind of Man* (1928) had signaled the "departure of the American factor analyists from the model provided by Spearman" (Jenkins and Patterson, 1961) with his presentation of evidence for group factors in intelligence as opposed to Spearman's common factor, *g*, it was Thurstone who developed the first practicable multiple-factor methods that provided evidence supporting Thorndike's multifactor theory of intelligence. Later, other major factor systems resembling Thurstone's methods to a greater or lesser degree were developed in Scotland by G. H. Thomson (*Factorial Analysis of Human Ability*, 1939) and in England by Cyril Burt (*Factors of the Mind*, 1941). However, Thurstone's methods have led in popularity to the present time, perhaps because they are less laborious than most but primarily because "they permit one to choose, from among an infinity of mathematically equivalent solutions, that one which seems to make the most psychological sense" (Tuddenham, 1962).

Intending at first to relate his multiple-factor analysis method to Spearman's theoretical conceptualization of intelligence, Thurstone found that Spearman's tetrad difference equation for a single common factor (Spearman, 1927) was simply a special case of his own multiple-group centroid method of factor analysis (Thurstone, 1933). With the development of this latter method, practicable application of factor analysis became feasible. According to Thurstone, Spearman's two-factor methods of factor analysis encounter difficulties in dealing with group factors (factors common to some, but not to all the variables) and more than one general factor. In contrast, he claimed that multiple-factor analysis imposes no restriction on the number of group and general factors. In his APA presidential address in 1933, Thurstone discussed some of the early results from using his multiple-group centroid method. He had analyzed 60 adjectives descriptive of human behavior and had found five factors. Perhaps, he suggested, this meant that it is possible to describe and to study the complexity and variety of man along only five dimensions. More work was needed before very definite statements could be made. However, these results gave an inkling of the contributions which might be expected through use of the method of multiple factor analysis.

The following year (c. 1934), Thurstone launched another experimental attack on the structure of intelligence. Fifty-seven tests sampling intellectual functioning were administered to 240 students in the eighth grade, high school, and college. From this beginning, the Thurstones collaborated on the construction of a series of tests which were intended to measure the commonalities of intelligence, i.e., the *Primary Mental Abilities.* Theoretically based upon Thorndike's original notion that intelligence is comprised of a large number of relatively independent specific mental abilities, the work of the Thurstones during the 1930's and 1940's focused upon experimentally identifying and measuring these primary mental abilities in order to verify their theoretical framework. Progress was reported from time to time through the publication of numerous articles and books that included the *Theory of Multiple Factors* (Thurstone, 1933), *Vectors of the Mind* (Thurstone, 1935), *Primary Mental Abilities* (Thurstone, 1938), *Factorial Studies of Intelligence* (Thurstone and Thurstone, 1941) and *Multiple Factor Analysis* (Thurstone, 1948).

The resultant experimental test battery, the *Primary Mental Abilities* (PMA), consisted finally of 17 tests arranged in six test booklets, each representative of essentially one primary factor: memory, verbal comprehension, reasoning (principally induction), word fluency, number and space. Two additional factors, perceptual speed and deduction, were regarded by the authors as not sufficiently clear for general application. The experimental edition of the PMA was printed in 1941 and was administered to Chicago school children in grades 5 through 12 for the purpose of standardization and norming. In 1946, Thurstone and Thurstone published the first edition of the *Primary Mental Abilities,* a single test for general use. Two subsequent revised editions of the PMA were published by Thelma Thurstone in 1958 and in 1962 after the death of her husband.

Compromise, Contradictions, and Consensus

In 1940, Cyril Burt demonstrated that the results of any one factor analysis can be transformed easily into the results of another. Hence, the disagreement between Spearman and Thurstone about the structure of intelligence was shown to be largely a product of two different statistical methods. Spearman again acknowledged the existence of certain group factors and, when the correlations of Thurstone's primary factors themselves were factored, the major "second-order" factor to emerge bore remarkable resemblance to Spearman's general intellective factor, *g*. The Thurstone and Spearman conceptualizations appeared to be "not contradictory but merely alternative descriptions of the same set of relationships" (Tuddenham, 1962). As a result of what he found in his studies on the structure of intelligence, Burt (1940) favored the views of Spearman. One of Burt's findings was that structure seems to be a function of age. Although *g* appears to account for 50 percent of the variance in childhood, specific group factors contribute more to the variance as the person matures. This finding is in keeping with a generally accepted principle in developmental psychology, namely, that the pattern of growth tends to progress from general undifferentiated responses toward greater differentiation and specialization.

Spearman insisted that the Thurstone's second-order general factor was not "second-order" at all but was actually the same primary general factor he had been talking about for many years. Thurstone acknowledged that there is no single unique result from a factor-analytic study. In 1948, he explained that "first-order" factors represent primary abilities which function as media for the expression of intellect and which probably are connected with separate organs of the body. His second-order factors represented more central, universe parameters that influence the activities of the primary factors.

It became more and more evident to all concerned that factor analysis is an arbitrary method. G. H. Thomson, an internationally recognized expert on factor analysis, publicly expressed his doubts that the procedure had much value. W. Stephenson, another English expert, suggested that, rather than factor-analyzing tests, psychologists should factor analyze people by administering a large number of tests to a small number of persons in order to obtain the factor saturations for the individuals. In spite of all this, the search for factors or abilities went on.

Taking up where Thurstone left off, J. P. Guilford found *g*, verbal, numerical, spatial, memory, speed of perception, fluency, and alertness factors in intelligence and also uncovered some leads in the direction of others. By 1948, Guilford had identified 27 factors in human abilities. Among them were space (awareness of spatial arrangement in which reference to the body is important), visual memory, rote memory, reproductive memory, and mechanical knowledge.

Following his factor analytic investigations into the structure of intelligence, Guilford (1959) erected a theoretical model of intellect in the shape of a $5 \times 4 \times 6$ cube. He listed five major content factors, four mental operations factors and six products factors. He speculated that 120 unique abilities exist. However, Guilford's cube model was soon called into question when later studies revealed that some cells contained more than one factor. However, Guilford concluded that, in order to assess an individual thoroughly, many different scores would be required because a number of the factors may be intercorrelated.

In spite of the lengthy dialogue that has continued over the years since the turn of the century, many people regard the structure of intelligence to be, at least implicitly, congruent with Spearman's two-factor formulation. As elaborated by A. W. Stern in 1956, the primary mental factors may be thought to possess characteristics somewhat analogous to those of nuclear particles; i.e., they exhibit collective as well as independent behaviors and possess group as well as individual properties. Factor analytic studies of mental abilities have received their most important application in the increasing use of "multi-aptitude" test batteries for educational and vocational guidance. Although not developed factor analytically as were the Thurstones' PMA, the first such battery was the *Differential Aptitude Tests* (DAT, Bennett, Seashore, and Wesman, 1947–1963), composed of a series of separate tests suggested by the findings of factor analysis. Stressing the significance of *abilities* rather than *ability*, the DAT were purported to assess seven specific abilities of high school youth: Verbal Reasoning, Numerical Reasoning, Abstract Reasoning, Space Relations, Mechanical Reasoning, Clerical Speed and Accuracy, and Language Usage. Although not intended to be "pure" measures of independent mental factors, the DAT subtests were designed to provide a profile of an individual's relative strengths and weaknesses that would be more definitive, descriptive, and meaningful than an omnibus general mental ability measure.

Most test consumers seem to value a scale which yields a profile of mental abilities over one which furnishes a single estimate of intelligence. However, it would have been significant if one theory of the structure of intelligence had produced a scale which differed in structure from another, but this was not the case. Scales based upon Spearman's theory are just as capable of yielding a profile as Thurstone's *Primary Mental Abilities* or the *Differential Aptitude Tests*. Conversely, tests typical of the latter type appear saturated with *g*. It does not seem to make much difference, therefore, whether one subscribes to Spearman's or Thurstone's (or Guilford's) theory of intelligence. Consequently, the fine distinctions between a general factor and specific factors, as against specific factors and a second-order general factor, etc., has a subtlety that is unimpressive to those not personally involved in the dispute (Reisman, 1966).

Nature, Nurture, and Non-sequitur

Another topic of considerable interest was the issue of the extent to which human behavior is innate *versus* the extent to which it is acquired. With respect to intelligence, at one extreme were those who held that intellectual ability is almost entirely inherited. Therefore, certain races and ethnic groups cannot be expected to achieve the highest cultural levels because of their inherent limitations. At the other extreme were those who believed that intellectual ability is almost completely acquired. Therefore, healthy children of different races raised under identical environmental conditions could be expected to function identically in school. Most psychologists held positions less extreme than either of these and simply emphasized one of the major variables over the other.

One of the great changes of the 1920's was that, within the span of a few years, a large number of psychologists shifted from a nature to a nurture emphasis, thus denying racial and ethnic inherent inequalities. However, it remained clear that the environmental position was not sufficient to provide an explanation of all cases of mental subnormality. A synthesis between the nature-nurture positions was in order. Steps in effecting such a synthesis were taken throughout the 1930's. P. A. Witty and H. C. Lehman (1933) concluded that it is futile to attempt to dichotomize behavior into learned and innate categories. Most behaviors are due to interactions between heredity and environment, and both are essential to a full understanding of growth. The question of whether heredity or environment is more important has become a dead issue. In the course of time, the major question has become: How or in what way do heredity and environment influence an individual's functioning?

Readin', 'Ritin', 'n' 'Rithmetic Revisited

Store-Bought Products

Among the areas of human functioning which have been explored, that of school achievement has persisted in stimulating a high level of continued interest and productive work among measurement experts. The success of the Army examinations aroused interest in measuring the relationship between mental ability and academic achievement. The first test to attempt this measurement was the *Illinois Examination* developed by W. S. Monroe and B. R. Buckingham in 1919, revised and published in 1920. Designed for grades 3–8, this test was organized in two separate parts: Part I consisted of an ordinary scholastic ability measure, the *Illinois General Intelligence Scale* (Monroe and Buckingham, 1919, revised 1920); Part II contained two school achievement tests, the Monroe *General Survey Scale in Arithmetic* (1920b) and the Monroe *Standardized Silent Reading Tests, revised* (1920a). The two parts were kept distinct when the scale was scored. Mental age norms were provided for the intelligence score, and achievement age norms were published for a composite achievement test score. The latter norms were established as the median composite test score made by pupils of a given mental age. Mental age scores were expressed in terms of standard deviation units. A pupil's achievement age was divided by his mental age to provide an *achievement quotient* (AQ), defined as the ratio between what the pupil achieved and what it is assumed he should be able to accomplish on the basis of his intelligence rating.

A similar concept was derived independently by Raymond Franzen (1920) and by W. A. McCall (1920) and was called an *accomplishment quotient,* or *educational quotient* (EQ). Both the achievement quotient and the accomplishment quotient "produced numerically identical results" (Monroe, 1923). They differed in that Monroe's quotient was based upon mental age norms, while Franzen and McCall employed chronological age norms. The Franzen or McCall method was simpler than Monroe's approach. Nevertheless, both quotients and other similar techniques eventually fell into general disrepute as a result of adverse findings in studies such as those reported by E. E. Cureton (1937), Lida Haggerty (1941), and F. Tsao (1943).

What appeared to be the beginning of a trend toward building both mental ability and academic achievement tasks into one short test instrument gained little momentum. None of these instruments ever became popular, and, with the exception of the *Otis Classification Test* (1923–1941), they soon disappeared from the test scene. School personnel preferred to measure mental ability and school achievement by means of separate instruments. Moreover, the beginning of different, and badly needed, trends in achievement measurement had appeared at the same time as had the combined ability-achievement instruments. These innovations were to be far more attractive to school personnel because of their greater potential utility for educational guidance than was provided by the ability-achievement dual instrument.

Earlier standardized tests of achievement had been a survey type that afforded a generalized measure of a pupil's attainment in a given subject but had not provided the detailed information required for remedial work. Although a few of the earlier tests had been of good quality, the rush to publish and profit resulted in a flood of tests that were constructed hastily, standardized inadequately, and imperfect technically. Tests in the various subject-matter areas had been constructed independently of each other by different persons at different times and in different places. Norms for each test had been based upon different groups of children in different schools at various periods of the school year. Rarely were adequate descriptions given of the types and geographic distribution of the schools employed. It was impossible to measure educational progress reliably over a period of time, because usually only one form of a test was available. Furthermore, it was not possible to construct a profile of relative achievement in different subjects, because the norms provided with the different tests were not comparable.

E. L. Thorndike (1922) described this situation somewhat more picturesquely when he wrote:

> In the elementary schools we now have many inadequate and even fantastic procedures parading behind the banner of educational science. Alleged measurements are reported and used which measure the fact in question about as well as the noise of the thunder measures the voltage of the lightning. To nobody are such (procedures) more detestable than to the scientific worker with educational measurements.

Although Thorndike's comments focused upon educational measurement in the elementary schools, they were equally applicable to the secondary school level. About the same time as these comments were expressed, however, efforts were begun toward the view of bringing some order into this chaos. Test makers instituted two new directions in educational achievement measurement: (1) the development of diagnostic tests in various subject fields, whose function was to provide specific information concerning a pupil's academic strengths and weaknesses; and (2) the development of school achievement batteries consisting of survey tests in the more important school subjects, all devised by the same author(s) and published as a single test instrument.

Of the many educational tests developed during the 1920's that were alleged to have utility for diagnostic purposes, by careful study few could provide evidence for substantiating these claims. Among the post-war tests listed by G. M. Ruch and G. D. Stoddard (1927) as meeting, to some degree, criteria for genuine diagnostic value were Ruch's own *Compass Diagnostic Tests in Arithmetic* (1925) for grades 5–8, the *Douglas Diagnostic Tests for 1st Year Algebra* (1921, revised 1923), the *Henmon Latin Test* (1921), the *Pressey-Richards American History Test* (1922) for grades 6–12, S. L. Pressey's *Diagnostic Tests in English Composition* (1923) for grades 7–12, and the *Van Wagenen English Composition Scales* (1923) for grades 4–12. Many other tests were developed over the next twenty years that were professed to diagnose difficulties associated with learning the three R's or specific subject-matter content. Most of these tests were limited to the tool subjects at the elementary school level.

A major problem associated with diagnostic tests was that scarcely one of them provided as much reliable information as was needed for effective diagnosis in any academic field. This and other problems associated with diagnostic tests and their interpretation remain a major concern of educational measurement. Measurement experts have been in general agreement that diagnosis is a very important function of educational measurement in every subject at all levels. The function of educational diagnosis is to determine the nature and causes of unsatisfactory adjustment to the school situation for the purpose of correcting and preventing maladjustment. The modern concept of education demands that a more comprehensive knowledge of the life behavior of a child be obtained in order to effect the understanding necessary to help that child gain maximum benefit from the experience of school. Current extensive research in this direction holds promise for the future.

The first scientific workers to attempt to bring order into the post-World War I achievement test chaos were T. L. Kelley, G. M. Ruch, and L. M. Terman with their development of the pioneer *Stanford Achievement Test* (1923). Although the organization of different subject-matter tests into a single instrument had been undertaken as early as 1920 by such men as Rudolf Pintner and J. C. Chapman, their instruments surveyed only the reading and arithmetic subject-matter areas. The *Stanford Achievement Test* was the first instrument that properly could be classified as a test *battery*. Its authors' goal was:

> . . . to construct a battery of tests which would cover practically all the curriculum from grades II to VIII, which would be easy to administer, which would not be too time-consuming, which would yield consistent results, and which would have the greatest possible validity as a basis for the grading and classification of pupils. (Ruch and Stoddard, 1927)

Although the use of standardized tests as a basis for grading pupils in school was discredited eventually as a valid purpose for standardized testing, in general, the other objectives of the Stanford authors were achieved by their test battery. Tests in reading (Word Meaning, Sentence Meaning, and Paragraph Meaning), arithmetic (Arithmetic Computation and Arithmetic Reasoning), Language Usage, and Spelling comprised the elementary battery for grades 2–3. The advance battery for grades 4–9 included two additional tests: (1) History and Literature Information and (2) Nature Study and Science Information. Two forms, purported to be equivalent, were prepared for each level. The administration of the test presented no difficulty, and scoring was objective. Approximately 80 minutes were required for administering the elementary battery, and 140 minutes were required for the advance battery. Extensive normative data were provided, including norms for each sub test, which enabled the computation of a pupil's "subject age" and general educational age (EA). In addition, provision was made for constructing pupil profiles of relative achievement in various subjects. Reliability coefficients, based upon data obtained from a sample of 1204 pupils in grades 2–9, were estimated separately for the sub tests and for the entire battery for each age from age 7 to age 15.

The first extensive revision of the *Stanford Achievement Test* was published in 1929. Five forms were prepared for each level of the battery in order to permit not only the construction of pupil profiles but also the measurement of progress over time. A later battery, similar to the Stanford in terms of both content and high quality of test construction, was the *Metropolitan Achievement Tests* (Hildreth, *et al.*, 1931–1947; Durost, *et al.*, 1958–1962). Both batteries have been revised several times over the years and have retained a position of prominence among the leaders in their field.

Home-Made Jobs

Dating from an initial study made by Max Meyer (1908), which emphasized the need for reform in college marking, the results of numerous studies focused upon the unreliability of school marks and examinations and seriously undermined the confidence previously placed in classroom teachers' measurement and evaluation procedures. Without exception, studies on the reliability of school grades had demonstrated that school marks were highly subjective, a function more of the personality of the teacher than of the performance of the student. Moreover, evidence from studies on school examinations, such as the dramatic study by Daniel Starch and Edward C. Elliott (1913), was even more damaging. Prior to World War I, evidence from both types of studies had served as a very strong stimulus for the development of standardized tests. However, its impact upon the everyday practices of the classroom teacher was delayed.

A number of textbooks on measurement were published during the 1920's which reflected a growing demand for higher standards in evaluating the products of the classroom: W. A. McCall's *How to Measure in Education* (1922), a comprehensive and critical book on achievement tests; Ben D. Wood's *Measurement in Higher Education* (1923), the first treatise on measurement at the college level; and G. M. Ruch's *The Improvement of the Written Examination* (1924), the first book devoted wholly to the "new-type" examination proposed by McCall (1920) for teachers' own classroom tests.

McCall's 1920 article, "A new kind of school examination," appeared in the very first issue of the *Journal of Educational Research*, a journal that immediately began to have a strong influence upon the educational measurement movement. McCall proposed that classroom teachers should employ the same objective item forms in their own examinations that were being used in standardized tests. Although many educators were wary of scientific measurement, the more progressive among them in time began to question the validity of their traditional practices:

> It is only yesterday that it occurred to most of us that there might be skilled techniques of testing or that the uses we were accustomed to make of our tests and examinations might be open to question. Every teacher or administrator of more than twenty years' service will recall with me that Age of Innocence when a "test" regularly consisted of ten questions, sometimes concocted impromptu as we wrote them on the blackboard, each weighted, by our arbitrary personal fiat, with a value of 10 on a scale of 100, and when the perfectly simple purpose of any "test" was to "pass" or "flunk" the testees. . . . It was only after the World War that this primal innocence was disturbed by . . . "the new tests." (McConn, 1935)

The "new" type of examination became popular quickly during the 1920's and, unfortunately, often was used uncritically. In order to foster the proper adoption by classroom teachers of the objective measurement principles advocated by measurement experts, many new books, monographs, and hundreds of articles were published on the various phases of measurement and their applications to educational assessment. In 1927, five important books on measurement were published. P. M. Symond's *Measurement in Secondary Education* and G. M. Ruch and G. D. Stoddard's *Tests and Measurements in High School Instruction* were the first two books specifically devoted to measurement in the high school. Truman Kelley produced his *Interpretation of Educational Measurements,* which remained for many years the most critical discussion available on certain technical aspects of measurement. It was also in this same year that Thorndike's *The Measurement of Intelligence* and Spearman's *The Abilities of Man* appeared, each representing a distinct point of view that exerted profound influence upon the measurement movement in general. The following year, in 1928, Clark Hull's critical volume *Aptitude Testing* was published, which remained the most complete discussion of that topic for a number of years.

Critical Caution

Beginning in the late 1920's, an increasing emphasis upon the limitations of measurement was reflected in the literature. Not only was emphasis placed upon limitations associated with testing instruments themselves, but also attention was directed to the human element in the test situation. In 1935, A. S. Barr stated well the principal limitation of measurement due to human factors or the "personal equation:"

> The chief difficulty today lies, it seems, not so much in the inadequacy of our instruments as in the inadequacy of the persons who use them: their failure to choose measurements in terms of the specific purpose to be served; their use of instruments of measurement for purposes for which they were never intended; the neglect or nonmeasurement of products of instruction that cannot be measured objectively; their treatment of reliable instruments as if they were valid, etc. (In Woody, *et al.*, 1935)

In the 1930's, educational measurement moved from "adolescence into maturity" (Monroe, 1945). Test makers as a group no longer made the exaggerated claims for their products that were quite common the decade before. Educational measurement had reached a new stage of development, the *stage of critical caution.* Characterizing the entire measurement movement since the 1930's, this stage may be described as the product of continued experimentation that has resulted in more authoritative research findings and in more intelligent interpretation of test data. It became recognized that "tests are means and not ends, and that even the best test is but a tool, the value of which depends upon the skill and the intelligence with which it is used" (Ross, 1947). This momentum towards rigorous use of scientific method in the theory, precision, and usefulness of educational and psychological measurement was increased by the founding of two quarterly professional journals in the late 1930's and early 1940's: *Psychometrika,* "devoted to the development of psychology as a quantitative rational science;" and *Educational and Psychological Measurement,* "devoted to the development and application of measures of individual differences" (Stanley, 1964).

Largely as an outgrowth of the critical attitude toward tests represented in the literature on measurement, there grew the trend to extend the field of measurement into new areas and to develop new, usually more specific, types of tests. However, the eight-year study of the Progressive Education Association reported that educational measurement had overemphasized the testing of limited areas of knowledge and skills to the exclusion of other important educational objectives (Smith and Tyler, 1942). E. F. Lindquist and R. W. Tyler led a so-called "evaluation movement," the objective of which was to correct this state of affairs. In addition to emphasizing that existing testing devices neglected significant realms of student behavior, the evaluation movement led to a more adequate assessment of the higher mental processes, such as application and analysis, and of broad areas of non-intellectual skills and learnings, such as interests and attitudes.

A "New Look" for Achievement Tests

The *Iowa Every-Pupil Tests of Basic Skills* (1936–1963), developed by E. F. Lindquist (general editor) and his colleagues at the State University of Iowa, were designed to measure certain skills crucial to the whole educational development of the pupil that largely determine the extent to which the pupil can profit from later instruction. In other words, these test authors focused upon the measurement of educational objectives associated with understanding and application of knowledge, rather than recall of subject-matter facts. Organized into two batteries for grades 3–5 and 6–9, the *Iowa Every-Pupil Tests of Basic Skills* provided separate tests in reading, vocabulary, work-study, language, and arithmetic skills that analyzed and sampled a large number (23) of skills in these four areas. Item content was no longer tied to the specific content of textbooks in a subject field. Tables classifying test items according to the specific skills measured provided an invaluable aid to the diagnosis of individual difficulties.

The Iowa authors presented an excellent discussion of validity, reliability, and standardization data in the *Manual for Administration and Interpretation* (1937), including a detailed description of how to use the four sets of available norms: grade, percentile, age-at-grade, and chronological age. Moreover, wise precautions for interpreting scores, valuable suggestions for remedial instruction, and sound teaching suggestions for developing each of the component skills were included in the manual. An ingenious feature of the 1937 form of this test battery was its use of a novel stencil scoring key. When the publication of the 1940 revision of this Iowa battery was taken over by the Houghton Mifflin Company, the principal weaknesses of the earlier mimeographed editions (poor quality of paper and lack of legibility of print) were eliminated. Later revised and refined several times, the *Iowa Tests of Basic Skills* (1949–1964) have become a leader in their field and have been viewed to mark the beginning of a "new look" for achievement measurement: the focus upon the products of higher mental processes.

The immediate acceptance of this new trend was reflected in the work of other test authors. The 1938 revision of the *Progressive Achievement Tests* (Tiegs and Clark, 1933–1943), renamed the *California Achievement Tests* in later revisions, also were intended as an instrument for the diagnosis of pupil abilities in the tool subjects: reading, arithmetic, and language. A short time later, the "new look" was extended to secondary-school achievement testing. The *Iowa*

Tests of Educational Development (ITED), devised by K. W. Vaughn and his colleagues under the direction of Lindquist (1942), consisted of nine tests for grades 9–13. This battery was intended to measure the relatively permanent learnings effected in certain broad aspects of a student's educational development, rather than the specifics of particular courses. As in the case of the Iowa elementary battery, the construction and standardization of the ITED were executed with considerable care. In a similar fashion, the *Sequential Tests of Educational Progress,* developed in 1957 by the Cooperative Test Division of the Educational Testing Service, were designed to assess the development of skills in seven learning fields for pupils at various levels from Grade 4 through the sophomore year in college.

With the modification of the long and widely used *Metropolitan Achievement Tests* (1958 revision) and the *Stanford Achievement Test* (1964 revision), all the major achievement tests now in common use reflect the Iowa basic skills model. Moreover, beginning with Thorndike's CAVD scale (1927) for which ability was described specifically as achievement, group intelligence tests have emphasized a similar convergent focus. Thus, while achievement batteries were being developed to diagnose pupil abilities in the basic skills associated with school learning, the trend in intelligence testing has been to interpret the results of mental ability tests as expressions of school achievement.

Beyond the New Horizon

With the general acceptance of the concepts that intelligence may be judged only by measuring its product and that intelligence and personality are inseparably bound together, the dimensions of human behavior with which measurement has become directly concerned include not only intelligence and achievement but also special abilities, personality, interests, attitudes, and social behavior. By the mid-1950's, a prophecy voiced at the time of the first world war appeared to be well on its way toward actualization. In 1917, C. H. Judd, a prominent educational psychologist and former student of E. L. Thorndike, decreed: ". . . the scope of measurement will be widened until it is sufficiently inclusive to satisfy even the most exacting critic" (Judd, 1918). With the advent of Sputnik in 1957, however, mental measurement met its most severe test.

The threat imposed by Russia's initial success in space led to a merciless attack upon the American educational system and, consequently, upon educational and psychological measurement. Shocked and bewildered, the American people were forced to recognize that Russian science and technology had stolen a march on American scientists and technologists in breaking the barriers of space. A sense of urgency prevailed that not only influenced the existing programs of scientific research toward the goal of strengthening the nation's military image but also inspired a movement to do something about scientific education on the theory that Russia was far ahead in the training of scientific personnel. For many, responsibility for the failure of the United States to take the initial lead in the exploration of space could be laid directly at the doorstep of the American educational system. The emphasis upon needing to improve scientific education was broadened to involve all aspects of education, including measurement of the outcomes of educational experiences.

Ironically, at the same time, educational and psychological measurement were attacked as devious methods for imposing conformity in thought and behavior, as invasions of privacy, and as obstacles that stood between an individual and the attainment of a worthwhile position in life. Nevertheless, demands increased for the development of more exacting instruments to measure man's social, political, and economic behavior. As a result of the National Defense Educational Act, research activity increased in both the development of new techniques of measurement and the revision of existing instruments. Moreover, increased efforts have been expended to promote informed, intelligent use of tests and other measurement techniques and to educate the general public toward better understanding of measurement.

Modern mental measurement is the product of a delayed conception, a prolonged gestation, a labored birth, an insecure infancy, a difficult childhood, and a turbulent adolescence. During this development, mental measurement has been feared and criticized by some, exploited and used in ignorance by others, and nurtured and defended by only a few. Still young, but seasoned by years of service demanded for both war and peace, measurement at last may have attained a long awaited maturity.

4

Promise and Prophecy

At the turn of the last century, James McKeen Cattell's pioneer effort to predict the academic performance of students at Columbia University was shown to be a failure. Alfred Binet was in the midst of his explorations which led to the development of an instrument that could distinguish between children capable of functioning in the regular classrooms in Paris, France, and children in need of what today would be termed special education. With the possible exception of a standardized spelling test developed during the late 1800's and used in parts of Massachuetts, no objectively scored standardized test of academic achievement of any description then existed.

During the three score and seven years that have intervened, successful methodologies for assessing the academic potential and achievement of children and adults have been developed, refined, and extended, so that very few adult persons living in the United States in 1968 have not completed one or more such measures. Today, complex theories, elaborate classification schemata, numerous books and articles relevant to the topics of statistics, test construction, test use, test interpretation, and fantastic electronic data processing installations exist and find wide acceptance and application.

The rapid growth of testing in American society has been a result of a combination of cultural forces which brought about the beginnings of extensive group testing by the military, educational institutions, government, and industry. In addition to the development of the necessary statistical and methodological technology, the acceptance by society of this innovation was dependent upon several factors. The most important cultural change which contributed both to the development of systematic measures of ability and achievement and to their popular acceptance was the realization that differences do exist between individuals. In combination with the traditional American values of achievement and mobility, this realization provided the ground work for a shift from the old ways of assigning status in the society, e.g., family background and race, to a new criterion: test performance. The speed of this transition was influenced strongly by the course of events in the first half of the 20th century: (1) the manpower allocation problems created by World War I and World War II; (2) the influx of immigrants prior to 1921; (3) the growing concern with the efficiency of our system of public education; (4) the increasing technological complexity of American society which made necessary better ways of identifying talented individuals to fill the specialized requirements of new jobs; and (5) the extraordinary growth of government which has created large civil service manpower demands (Goslin, 1963).

No test, scale, or other device can be thought of as yielding an absolutely true measure of any human attribute. Rather, at best, these instruments should be considered tools for providing useful information, on the basis of which it is possible to describe and predict human behavior. Prior to the "measure knowledge for use" innovations in achievement testing introduced by E. F. Lindquist, et al., a clear distinction could be made between measures of academic achievement and measures of mental ability. From the beginning, mental ability measures included novel item content which demanded that examinees use what knowledge they possessed, rather than merely remember what it was they knew. The difference between the two types of tests is now more difficult to discern. With respect to reliability of measurement, adequacy of norms, and validity of prediction, those measures that receive the widest use function with similar efficiency. At their best, measures of mental ability and academic achievement are representative of the most advanced psychometric work accomplished to date by anyone, anywhere.

The bulk of these measures are highly verbal in nature and place a premium upon an examinee's ability to demonstrate proficiency in academic skills learned in the classroom. Persons from white, urban, middle or upper socioeconomic class backgrounds are advantaged when confronted by such tests, because the content of these measures is drawn largely from those school experiences especially peculiar to these groups in American society. The more disparate a socioeconomic group may be in comparison to the white, urban middle-class norm, the less prob-able it is that individuals drawn from a disparate group have shared the experiences necessary to perform well upon these tests. Based upon mental ability or academic achievement measures alone, inferences as to the capacities or abilities of such individuals are ill-founded. None-theless, these measures do provide an index of an individual's prepara-tion for both academic accomplishment and the type of work de-manded by a modern technical society.

To date, literally hundreds of different group-administered tests of mental ability and academic achievement have been developed, pub-lished, and sold. The number of copies of such tests consumed over the years runs well into the tens of millions. Buros (1961) listed 2,126 tests in print. Moreover, innumerable tests have been developed by public and private organizations which never found their way into a bibliographic listing. Today, however, only a handful of this large number of different tests is in widespread use.

Most mental ability measures and academic achievement tests were designed to permit school personnel to administer and score the tests and to record the results. Proper interpretation of results does require some basic training in standardized testing, but not so much training that ample personnel should not be available in most schools to inter-pret and communicate results effectively to all persons legitimately concerned with these data.

At least three-quarters of the public school systems in the United States and a large proportion of the independent schools have regular interval testing programs. Most of the remainder make use of tests to some extent. More than a dozen national school or college testing programs are currently in existence, in addition to external testing programs sponsored by numerous state and local agencies. Internal testing programs occur somewhat more frequently at the elementary grade levels, while external testing is more typical of the programs em-ployed throughout junior high school, high school, and college. Test-ing frequently plays an important part in a wide range of decisions which may affect critically the lives of the nation's youth.

Industrial and business testing occupies a somewhat uncertain posi-tion in personnel management. The problem of predicting high level executive performance with either personality or ability tests has not been solved satisfactorily. Although interested parties have been chal-lenged by these difficulties, approaches to tentative solutions to the problem have been unsystematic and uncoordinated. In the areas where testing in industry is based upon a more firm ground, i.e., in the measurement of specific abilities and skills, organized labor has slowed down the application of existing testing technology. While standardized tests are being administered in larger and larger numbers, in some instances tests are used in accordance with the philosophy that "they won't do any harm." In such instances, the scores frequently are disregarded. A contributing factor to this state of affairs seems to be a relative lack of communication throughout the industrial and business world concerning new developments in selection techniques and a lack of coordination in the research being done.

In government personnel selection, many of the problems facing administrators are similar to those encountered by academic admissions officers and industrial personnel specialists. Defining the qualifications necessary for maximum performance, developing a reliable and valid measure of those qualifications or abilities, and finding the trained personnel to administer and interpret tests are the main stumbling blocks encountered by all test users. In addition to these standard difficulties, the problem of attracting sufficient numbers of qualified applicants to make a competitive examining system meaningful remains to be solved by merit system administrators.

The uses of objective tests by the armed forces may be divided into four main categories: (1) screening in induction, enlistment, and re-enlistment; (2) initial and continued classification of enlisted personnel; (3) selection and assignment of personnel for officer training; and (4) special selection and assignment of personnel for specific military jobs or military job training. In most cases, an individual's test score is not the sole determining factor for a member of the armed forces being accepted, rejected, or classified. However, because of the magnitude of the selection problem faced by the armed forces, the number of different jobs, and the number of candidates for these jobs, tests play a considerably greater role in military personnel allocation than in other occupational areas of American society at the present time.

When a field as technical as that of mental testing becomes so widely applied that it has tremendous impact upon the lives of so many people, it is not surprising to find a number of well-meaning persons offering criticisms which sometimes present a distorted picture of the place and value of ability and achievement testing.

> When carefully extricated from the emotional overtones in which they are all too often shrouded, most current criticisms of testing amount to statements that the accuracy of tests is not perfect, that many important attributes are not yet measured, that the use of tests is a cold, machine-like process and that the results of tests are sometimes misused. (Helmstadter, 1964)

No test specialist would contend that the measures now available provide a complete and precise description or prediction of an individual's behavior. Rather, tests are seen as devices with varying degrees of usefulness for providing the basis for informed decisions by and about people. Moreover, few specialists would claim that all important human characteristics can be assessed with present instruments. Many important human attributes thus far have eluded those who seek ways to describe individuals in quantitative terms.

Critics who charge that testing will lead to less, rather than to more, humane treatment of individuals are concerned without cause. Each person is truly a unique and complex individual. To study him, therefore, requires complicated ideas, complicated instruments, and complicated procedures. However, tests, like all other tools, which man has invented, can be and are being misused. There are those who forget, or fail to understand, the probabilistic nature of inferences derived from test scores and view such scores to be absolute indices of human attributes. The problem is one of education, i.e., restricting the use of tests to those persons who are willing to take the trouble to understand them and to use them in an informed fashion. Our knowledge of testing today is vast. However, the basic concepts, even though complex, are neither too many nor too difficult to learn for persons properly motivated. Hope lies in research rather than invective, in careful evaluation instead of emotional outburst, and in a realization that while we have come a long way, there is an even greater distance to go.

Test users need to apply high standards of professional judgment in selecting and interpreting tests, and test producers are under obligation to produce tests which can be of the greatest possible service. Commercial test publishers and distributors have taken over a large part of the responsibility for the development of accurate instruments. Consequently, the test producer has the particular task of providing sufficient information about each test in order that test consumers will know what degree of reliance can be placed upon it safely.

Professional workers agree that test manuals and associated aids to test users should be made complete, comprehensive, and unambiguous. For many years, publishers and authors of tests have adopted standards for themselves, and standards have been proposed in textbooks and other publications. Through the application of such standards, the best tests have attained a high degree of quality and usefulness. Until 1954, no statement represented a consensus concerning what information is most helpful to the test consumer. In the absence of such a guide, it was inevitable that some tests appeared with less adequate supporting information than did others of the same type.

To meet this need, the *Technical Recommendations for Psychological Tests and Diagnostic Techniques* was issued in March, 1954, by the American Psychological Association. In addition to this document, the *Technical Recommendations for Achievement Tests* was prepared and published in January, 1955, through the joint efforts of the American Educational Research Association and the National Council on Measurement in Education. In view of the similarity of many problems in both educational and psychological measurement, a joint committee representing all of the organizations noted above decided that it was advantageous to issue one set of standards for both educational and psychological tests. This joint effort resulted in the 1966 publication of the *Standards for Educational and Psychological Tests and Manuals*. A primary intent of the recommendations was to assist test producers to develop a wide variety of worthwhile and relevant tests.

What of the future and the challenge it affords? A perspective of mental measurement both past and present suggests that its future impact and value in American society may be very great indeed.

> For those who have an interest in studying and working with human beings, for those who are willing and diligent enough to examine complex concepts both through verbal and mathematical analysis and for those who can find creative solutions to seemingly impossible problems, there are thrilling prospects in store in the field of psychometrics. (Helmstadter, 1964)

This promise for the future may be fulfilled only if test producers and test consumers today, heeding the voices from the past, work together to produce creative and technically competent innovations in test development, selection, and use.

BIBLIOGRAPHY

American Educational Research Association, *Technical Recommendations for Achievement Tests*. Washington, D.C.: National Education Association, 1955.

American Psychological Association, *Technical Recommendations for Psychological Tests and Diagnostic Techniques*. Washington, D.C.: American Psychological Association, 1954.

American Psychological Association, American Educational Research Association, and National Council on Measurement in Education, *Standards for Educational and Psychological Tests and Manuals*. Washington, D.C.: American Psychological Association, 1966.

Anastasi, Anne, *Psychological Testing*, 2nd ed. New York: Macmillan, 1961.

Arthur, Grace, "The re-standardization of a point performance scale." *Journal of Applied Psychology*, Vol. 12, 1928, pp. 278–303.

Ashbaugh, E. J., "Cooperative work from a university center." *Seventeenth Yearbook, National Society for the Study of Education*, Vol. 17, 1918, pp. 57–70.

Ayres, L. P., *Ayres' Scale for Measuring the Quality of Handwriting of Adults*. New York: Russell Sage Foundation, 1912a.

———, *Ayres' Spelling Scale*. New York: Division of Education, Russell Sage Foundation, 1915a.

———, "History and present status of educational measurements." *Seventeenth Yearbook, National Society for the Study of Education*, Vol. 17, 1918, pp. 9–15.

———, *Laggards in Our Schools*. New York: Russell Sage Foundation, 1909.

———, "Measuring educational processes through educational results." *School Review*, Vol. 20, 1912b, pp. 300–309.

———, *A Measuring Scale for Ability in Spelling*. New York: Division of Education, Russell Sage Foundation, 1915b.

———, "Psychological tests in vocational guidance." *Journal of Educational Psychology*, Vol. 4, 1913, pp. 232–237.

———, ed., *The Cleveland Education Survey* (25 volumes). Cleveland, Ohio: Cleveland Education Survey Committee, 1915–1916.

———, *The Public Schools of Springfield, Illinois.* New York: Russell Sage Foundation, 1914.

Bagley, W. C., "On the correlation of mental and motor ability in school children." *American Journal of Psychology*, Vol. 12, 1900, pp. 193–205.

Bain, A., *The Senses and the Intellect.* London: Parker, 1895.

Baker, H. J., *Detroit Intelligence Test.* Bloomington, Illinois: Public School Publishing Company, 1927.

Barr, A. S., *Diagnostic Tests in American History.* Bloomington, Illinois: Public School Publishing Company, 1918.

Bennett, G. K., Seashore, H. G., and Wesman, A. G., *Differential Aptitude Tests.* New York: The Psychological Corporation, 1947–1963.

Bennett, G. K., et al., *Academic Promise Tests.* New York: The Psychological Corporation, 1961–1962.

Bennett, G. K., et al., *College Qualification Tests.* New York: The Psychological Corporation, 1958–1961.

Binet, A., " Double consciousness in health." *Mind*, Vol. 15, 1890, pp. 46–57.

———, *The Experimental Study of Intelligence.* Paris: Schleicher, 1902.

———, *The Psychology of Reasoning.* Paris: Alcan, 1886.

———, and Fore, C., *Animal Magnetism.* New York: Appleton, 1888.

———, and Henri, V., "Individual psychology." *L'Année Psychologie*, Vol. 2, 1896, pp. 411–463.

———, and Simon, T., "The development of intelligence in children." *L'Année Psychologie*, Vol. 14, 1908, pp. 1–90.

———, *The Development of Intelligence in Children.* Translated by Elizabeth S. Kite. Baltimore, Maryland: Williams and Wilkins, 1916.

———, "New methods for the diagnosis of the intellectual level of subnormals." *L'Année Psychologie*, Vol. 11, 1905a, pp. 191–244.

———, "Upon the necessity of establishing a scientific diagnosis of inferior states of intelligence." *L'Année Psychologie*, Vol. 11, 1905b, pp. 163–191.

———, and Vaschide, N., "Psychology of the primary school." *L'Année Psychologie*, Vol. 2, 1896, pp. 411–465.

Bingham, W. V. D., et al., (Personnel Research Section, Adjutant General's Office), *Army General Classification Test* (first civilian edition). Chicago, Illinois: Science Research Associates, 1947.

Boas, F., "Anthropological investigations in schools." *Pedagogical Seminary*, Vol. 1, 1891, pp. 13–18.

Bolton, T. L., "Growth of memory in school children." *American Journal of Psychology*, Vol. 4, 1892, pp. 362–380.

Book, W. F., *The Intelligence of High School Seniors.* New York: Macmillan, 1922.

Boring, E. G., "The beginning and growth of measurement in psychology." *Isis*, Vol. 52, 1961, pp. 238–257.

————, *The History of Experimental Psychology*. New York: Appleton-Century-Crofts, Inc., 1950.

————, *et al.*, eds., *A History of Psychology in Autobiography*, Volume IV. Worcester, Massachusetts: Clark University Press, 1952.

Bregman, Elsie O., and Cattell, J. M., *Revision of Army Alpha Examination*. New York: The Psychological Corporation, 1925 and 1935.

Brett, G. S., *A History of Psychology* (Volume I). London: Allen, 1912.

————, *A History of Psychology* (Volume II). New York: Macmillan, 1921.

Brigham, C. C., *A Study of American Intelligence*. Princeton, New Jersey: Princeton University Press, 1923.

Bryner, Edna, "A selected bibliography of certain phases of educational measurement." *Seventeenth Yearbook, National Society for the Study of Education*, Vol. 17, 1918, pp. 161–190.

Buckingham, B. R., *Extension of the Ayres Spelling Scale*. Urbana, Illinois: Bureau of Educational Research, 1916.

————, "Our first twenty-five years." *Proceedings of the National Education Association*, 1941, p. 354.

————, *Scale for Problems in Arithmetic*. Bloomington, Illinois: Public School Publishing Company, 1919.

————, *Spelling Ability: Its Measurement and Distribution*. New York: Teachers' College, Columbia University, 1913.

Burks, Barbara S., Jensen, Dortha W., and Terman, L. M., *Genetic Studies of Genius: III. The promise of youth: followup studies of a thousand gifted children*. Palo Alto, California: Stanford University Press, 1930.

Buros, O. K., *Educational, Psychological, and Personality Tests of 1933, 1934, and 1935*. New Brunswick, New Jersey: Rutgers University Press, 1936.

————, ed., *Tests in Print*. Highland Park, New Jersey: Gryphon Press, 1961.

Burt, C., "Experimental tests of higher mental processes and their relation to general intelligence." *Journal of Experimental Pedagogy*, Vol. 1, 1911, pp. 93–112.

————, *The Factors of the Mind*. London: University of London Press, 1940.

————, *Mental and Scholastic Tests*. London: Staples, 1947.

Caldwell, O. P., and Courtis, S. A., *Then and Now in Education, 1845–1923*. New York: World Book Company, 1925.

Cattell, J. M., "Address of the President before the American Psychological Association, 1895." *Psychological Review*, Vol. 3, 1896, pp. 134–148.

————, "The conception and methods of psychology." *Popular Science Monthly*, Vol. 66, 1904, pp. 173–186.

————, "Early psychological laboratories." *Science*, Vol. 67, 1928, pp. 543–548.

————, "Mental tests and measurements." *Mind,* Vol. 15, 1890, pp. 373–381.

————, "Psychology in America." *Scientific Monographs,* Vol. 30, 1930, pp. 114–126.

————, and Farrand, L., "Physical and mental measurements of the students of Columbia University." *Psychological Review,* Vol. 3, 1896, pp. 618–648.

Cattell, Psyche, *Infant Intelligence Scale.* New York: The Psychological Corporation, 1940a.

————, *The Measurement of Intelligence of Infants and Young Children.* New York: The Psychological Corporation, 1940b.

Chadwick, E., "Statistics of educational research." *The Museum: A Quarterly Magazine of Education, Literature and Science,* Vol. 3, 1864, pp. 480–484.

Chapman, J. C., *Classroom Products Survey Test.* Philadelphia: J. B. Lippincott, 1920 (revised 1921).

Cole, L. W., and Vincent, Leona, *The Cole-Vincent Group Intelligence Tests for School Entrants.* Emporia, Kansas: Kansas State Teachers College of Emporia, Bureau of Educational Measurements, 1924–1928.

College Entrance Examination Board, *Scholastic Aptitude Tests.* Princeton, New Jersey: College Entrance Examination Board, 1925 (new forms each year thereafter).

Colvin, S. S., *Brown University Psychological Examination, Series II.* Philadelphia: J. B. Lippincott, 1920.

Cook, W. W., "Achievement tests." *Encyclopedia of Educational Research* (revised edition). New York: Macmillan, 1950, pp. 1461–1478.

Cooperative Test Division, *Cooperative School and College Ability Tests.* Princeton, New Jersey: Educational Testing Service, 1955.

————, *Cooperative Sequential Tests of Educational Progress.* Princeton, New Jersey: Educational Testing Service, 1957.

Cornman, O. P., *Spelling in the Elementary School: An Experimental and Statistical Investigation.* Boston: Ginn and Company, 1902.

Courtis, S. A., "Contributions of research to the individualization of instruction." *Thirty-seventh Yearbook, National Society for the Study of Education,* Vol. 37, 1938, pp. 201–210.

————, *Courtis Standard Practice Tests in Arithmetic, Series A.* New York: World Book Company, 1912.

————, *Courtis Standard Research Tests, Arithmetic, Series B.* Detroit, Michigan: S. A. Courtis, 1914.

————, "The Courtis tests in arithmetic." In Courtis, S. A., ed., *Final report, Educational Investigation Committee on School Inquiry,* Volume 1. New York: City of New York, 1911.

————, *The Gary Public Schools: Measurement of Classroom Products.* New York: General Education Board, 1919.

————, "Let's stop this worship of tests and scales." *Nation's Schools*, Vol. 31, 1943, pp. 16–17.

————, *Standard Tests in English, Series C.* Detroit, Michigan: Courtis Standard Tests, Department of Cooperative Research, 1913.

Cox, Catherine M., *Genetic Studies of Genius: II. The early mental traits of three hundred geniuses.* Palo Alto, California: Stanford University Press, 1926.

Cureton, E. E., "The accomplishment quotient technic." *Journal of Experimental Education*, Vol. 5, 1937, pp. 315–326.

Dearborn, W. F., *Dearborn Group Tests of Intelligence, Series I and Series II.* Philadelphia: J. B. Lippincott, 1920.

Division of Psychology, Medical Department, War Department. *Army Mental Tests, Methods, Typical Results and Practical Application.* Washington, D.C.: War Department, 1918.

Douglas, H. R., *Douglas Diagnostic Tests for 1st Year Algebra.* Cincinnati, Ohio: Bureau of Administrative Research, University of Cincinnati, 1921 (revised 1923).

Durost, W. N., ed., *Metropolitan Achievement Tests.* New York: Harcourt, Brace & World, 1958–1962.

Ebbinghaus, H., "Ueber eine neue methode zur prüfung geistiger fahigkeiten und ihre anwendung bei schulkindern." *Zeitschrift fur Psychologie*, Vol. 13, 1897, pp. 401–450.

Engel, Anna M., *Detroit First-Grade Intelligence Test.* New York: World Book Company, 1920 (revised 1921).

Englehart, M. D., and Thomas, M., "Rice as the inventor of the comparative test." *Journal of Educational Measurement*, Vol. 3, 1966, pp. 141–145.

Esquirol, J. E. D., *Medical, Therapeutic and Legal Considerations for Mental Illness.* Paris: Bailliere, 1838.

Fechner, G., *Elemente du Psychophysik.* Leipzig: Breitkoph and Härtel, 1860.

————, *Revision der Hauptpuncte der Psychophysik.* Leipzig: Breitkoph and Härtel, 1882.

Fernald, G. G., "Character vs. intelligence in personality studies." *Journal of Abnormal Psychology*, Vol. 15, 1920–1921, pp. 1–10.

Flugel, J. C., *A Hundred Years of Psychology: 1833–1933.* New York: Macmillan, 1933.

Franz, S. I., *Handbook of Mental Examination Methods.* New York: Macmillan, 1919.

Franzen, R., "The accomplishment quotient." *Teachers College Record*, Vol. 21, 1920, pp. 432–440.

Freeman, F. N., *Mental Tests: Their History, Principles, and Applications.* Boston: Houghton Mifflin, 1926.

Galton, F., "Co-relations and their measurement, chiefly from anthropometric data." *Proceedings of the Royal Society of London,* Vol. 16, 1888, pp. 135–145.

———, *Hereditary Genius: An Inquiry into its Laws and Consequences.* New York: D. Appleton and Company, 1869.

———, *Inquiries into Human Faculty and its Development.* London: Macmillan, 1883.

———, *Memories of My Life.* London: Methuen, 1908.

———, *Natural Inheritance.* New York: Macmillan, 1889.

———, "Psychometric experiments." *Brain,* Vol. 2, 1879, pp. 149–162.

Gesell, A., *The Mental Growth of the Preschool Child: a psychological outline of normal development from birth to the sixth year, including a system of developmental diagnosis.* New York: Macmillan, 1925a.

———, *Pre-school Child Test.* Chicago: C. H. Stoelting Company, 1925b.

———, and Amatruda, Catherine S., *Developmental Diagnosis: normal and abnormal child development, clinical methods, and practical applications.* New York: Paul B. Hoeber, Inc., 1941.

———, and Thompson, Helen (assisted by Catherine S. Amatruda), *The Psychology of Early Growth: including norms of infant behavior and a method of genetic analysis.* New York: Macmillan, 1938.

———, et al., *The First Five Years of Life: a guide to the study of the preschool child.* New York: Harper & Brothers, 1940.

Gilbert, J. A., "Researches on mental and physical development of school-children." *Studies from the Yale Psychological Laboratory,* Vol. 2, 1894, pp. 40–100.

———, "Researches upon school children and college students." *University of Iowa Studies in Psychology,* Vol. 1, 1897, pp. 1–39.

Goddard, H. H., "A measuring scale for intelligence." *The Training School,* Vol. 6, 1910, pp. 146–155.

———, "A revision of the Binet Scale." *The Training School,* Vol. 8, 1911b, pp. 56–62.

———, "Two thousand normal children measured by the Binet Measuring Scale of Intelligence." *Pedagogical Seminary,* Vol. 18, 1911a, pp. 232–259.

Goodenough, Florence L., *Mental Testing: Its History, Principles and Applications.* New York: Rinehart and Company, 1949.

———, Maurer, Katherine M., and Van Wagenen, M. J., *Minnesota Preschool Scales.* Minneapolis, Minnesota: Educational Test Bureau, 1932–1940.

Goslin, D., *Search for Ability.* New York: Russell Sage Foundation, 1963.

Graham, Patricia A., "Joseph Mayer Rice as a founder of the progressive education movement." *Journal of Educational Measurement,* Vol. 3, 1966, pp. 129–133.

Guilford, J. P., "Three faces of intellect." *American Psychologist*, Vol. 14, 1050, pp. 409–479.

Haggerty, Lida H., "An evaluation of the accomplishment quotient: a four-year study at the junior high school level." *Journal of Experimental Education*, Vol. 10, 1941, pp. 78–89.

Haggerty, M. E., *The Haggerty Intelligence Examination, Delta 1* and *Delta 2*. New York: World Book Company, 1919a.

———, *Virginia Public Schools Education Commission Report*. Richmond, Virginia: Public Schools, 1919b.

———, *et al.* (National Research Committee), *National Intelligence Tests, Scales A and B*. New York: World Book Company, 1920.

Hall, G. S., "Contents of children's minds." *Princeton Review*, Vol. 11, 1883, pp. 272–294.

———, *Founders of Modern Psychology*. New York: Appleton Company, 1912.

Hart, B., and Spearman, C., "General ability, its existence and nature." *British Journal of Psychology*, Vol. 5, 1912, pp. 51–84.

Hawkes, H. E., Lindquist, E. F., and Mann, C. R., *The Construction and Use of Achievement Examinations*. Boston: Houghton Mifflin, 1936.

Healy, W., "A pictorial completion test." *Psychological Review*, Vol. 21, 1914, pp. 189–203.

———, and Fernald, Grace M., "Tests for practical mental classification." *Psychological Monographs*, Vol. 13, No. 2, 1911.

Helmstadter, G. C., *Principles of Psychological Measurement*. New York: Appleton-Century-Crofts, 1964.

Henmon, V. A. C., and Nelson, M. J., *Henmon-Nelson Tests of Mental Ability*. Boston: Houghton Mifflin, 1931–1961.

Hildreth, Gertrude, "Applications of intelligence testing." *Review of Educational Research*, Vol. 5, 1935, pp. 199–214.

———, *Bibliography of Mental Tests and Rating Scales*. New York: The Psychological Corporation, 1933.

———, and Griffiths, Nellie, *Metropolitan Readiness Tests*. New York: World Book Company, 1933–1965.

———, *et al.*, *Metropolitan Achievement Tests*. New York: World Book Company, 1931–1947.

Hilgard, E. R., *Theories of Learning*. New York: Appleton-Century-Crofts, 1948.

Hillegas, M. B., *Hillegas' Scale for the Measurement of the Quality in English Composition for Young People*. New York: Bureau of Publications, Columbia University, 1912.

Holtz, H. G., "First-year algebra scales." *Teachers College Contributions to Education*, No. 90, 1918.

Horrocks, J. E., *Assessment of Behavior*. Columbus, Ohio: Charles E. Merrill Books, 1964.

Huarte de San Juan, J., *Exàmen de Ingenios.* Madrid: Baeza, 1575 and 1698.

Huey, E. B., "The Binet scale for measuring intelligence and retardation." *Journal of Educational Psychology,* Vol. 1, 1910, pp. 435–444.

Hull, C., *Aptitude Testing.* New York: World Book Company, 1928.

Irwin, J. O., "Correlation of methods in psychology." *British Journal of Psychology,* Vol. 25, 1934, pp. 86–91.

Itard, J. M. G., *The Wild Boy of Aveyron.* New York: Appleton-Century-Crofts, 1962.

James, W., *Principles of Psychology.* New York: Henry Holt & Company, 1890.

Jastrow, J., "American psychology in the '80's and '90's." *Psychological Review,* Vol. 50, 1943, pp. 65–67.

——, "Some anthropometric and psychologic tests on college students." *American Journal of Psychology,* Vol. 4, 1892, pp. 420–427.

Jenkins, J. J., and Patterson, D. G., eds., *Studies in Individual Differences.* New York: Appleton-Century-Crofts, 1961.

Judd, C. H., "Contributions of school surveys." *Fifteenth Yearbook, National Society for the Study of Education,* Vol. 15, 1914, pp. 9–20.

——, "A look forward." *Seventeenth Yearbook, National Society for the Study of Education,* Vol. 17, 1918, pp. 152–160.

——, *Measuring the Work of the Public Schools.* Cleveland, Ohio: The Survey Committee of the Cleveland Foundation, 1916.

——, *et al., Cleveland Survey Arithmetic Tests.* Detroit, Michigan: S. A. Courtis, 1916.

Kelley, T. L., *Crossroads in the Mind of Man: a study of differential mental abilities.* Palo Alto, California: Stanford University Press, 1928.

——, "Educational guidance: an experimental study in the analysis and prediction of high-school pupils." *Teachers College Contributions to Education, No. 71.* New York: Teachers College, Columbia University, 1914.

——, *Interpretation of Educational Measurements.* New York: World Book Company, 1927.

——, Ruch, G. M., and Terman, L. M., *Stanford Achievement Tests.* New York: World Book Company, 1923–1964.

Kelly, R. L., "Psychophysical tests of normal and abnormal children: a comparative study." *Psychological Review,* Vol. 10, 1903, pp. 345–372.

Kirkpatrick, E., "Individual tests of school children." *Psychological Review,* Vol. 7, 1900, pp. 274–280.

Knox, H. A., "A Scale based on the work at Ellis Island for estimating mental defect." *Journal of the American Medical Association,* Vol. 62, 1914, pp. 741–747.

Kohs, S. C., "The Binet-Simon measuring scale for intelligence: an annotated bibliography." *Journal of Educational Psychology,* Vol. 5, 1914, pp. 215–224, 279–290, 334–346.

————, *Intelligence Measurement: a psychological and statistical study based upon the Block-Design Tests.* New York: Macmillan, 1923.

Kraepelin, E., "Der psychologische versuch in der psychiatre." *Psychologie Arbeiten,* Vol. 1, 1895, pp. 1–91.

Kuhlmann, F. A., *A Handbook of Mental Tests.* Baltimore: Warwick & York, 1922.

————, "A revision of the Binet-Simon system for measuring the intelligence of children." *Journal of Psycho-Asthenics, Monograph Supplement,* Vol. 1, 1912, pp. 1–41.

————, and Anderson, Rose G., *Kuhlmann-Anderson Intelligence Test.* Princeton, New Jersey: Personnel Press, 1927–1963.

Lamke, T. A., and Nelson, M. J., *The Henmon-Nelson Tests of Mental Ability, Revised Edition.* Boston: Houghton Mifflin, 1957–58.

Lindquist, E. F., "Cooperative achievement testing." *Journal of Educational Research,* Vol. 28, 1935, pp. 511–520.

————, *Manual for Administration and Interpretation of 1937 Iowa Every-Pupil Tests of Basic Skills.* Iowa City, Iowa: State University of Iowa, Bureau of Educational Research and Service, 1937.

————, *et al., Iowa Tests of Basic Skills.* Boston: Houghton Mifflin, 1949–1963.

Lorge, I., Thorndike, R. L., and Hagen, Elizabeth, *Lorge-Thorndike Intelligence Tests, Multi-Level Edition.* Boston: Houghton Mifflin, 1964.

MacPhail, A. H., *The Intelligence of College Students.* Baltimore, Maryland: Warwick & York, 1924.

Mann, H., "Boston grammar and writing schools." *Common School Journal,* Vol. 7, 1845a, pp. 289–368.

————, "Report of the annual examining committee of the Boston grammar and writing schools." *Common School Journal,* Vol. 7, 1845b, pp. 326–336.

Maxfield, F. N., "Trends in testing intelligence." *Educational Research Bulletin,* Vol. 15, 1936, pp. 134–141.

McCall, W. A., *How to Measure in Education.* New York: Macmillan, 1922.

————, *Measurement.* New York. Macmillan, 1939.

————, "A new kind of school examination." *Journal of Educational Research,* Vol. 1, 1920, pp. 33–46.

McConn, M., "Examinations old and new: their use and abuses." *Educational Record,* Vol. 16, 1935, pp. 375–411.

Meyer, M., "The grading of students." *Science,* Vol. 28, 1908, pp. 243–250.

Miller, W. S., "The administrative use of intelligence tests in the high school." *Twenty-first Yearbook, National Society for the Study of Education,* Vols. 21–22, 1922–1923, pp. 189–222.

————, *Miller Analogies Test.* New York: World Book Company, 1926.

Mitchell, D., and Ruger, G. J., *Psychological Tests, Revised and Classified Bibliography.* New York: The Bureau of Educational Experiments, 1918.

Monroe, W. S., "A bibliography of standardized tests for the high school." *Journal of Educational Research,* Vol. 1, 1920a, pp. 149–153, 229–242, 311–320.

————, "Educational measurement in 1920 and 1945." *Journal of Educational Research,* Vol. 38, 1945, pp. 334–340.

————, "Existing tests and standards." *Seventeenth Yearbook, National Society for the Study of Education,* Vol. 17, 1918a, pp. 71–104.

————, *General Survey Scale in Arithmetic.* Bloomington, Illinois: Public School Publishing Company, 1920a (revised, 1920–1921).

————, "Hazards in the measurement of achievement." *School and Society,* Vol. 41, 1935, pp. 48–52.

————, "Improvement of instruction through the use of educational tests." *Journal of Educational Research,* 1920b, pp. 96–102.

————, *An Introduction to the Theory of Educational Measurements.* Boston: Houghton Mifflin, 1923.

————, "Monroe's standardized reading tests." *Journal of Educational Psychology,* Vol. 9, 1918b, pp. 303–312.

————, "Some trends in educational measurement." *Twenty-fourth Annual Conference on Educational Measurements.* Bloomington, Indiana: Indiana University, Bureau of Cooperative Research, 1937. (Bulletin of the School of Education, Indiana University, Vol. 13, No. 4, 1937.)

————, *Standardized Silent Reading Tests, Revised.* Bloomington, Illinois: Public School Publishing Company, 1920b.

————, *The Theory of Educational Measurement.* Boston: Houghton Mifflin, 1923.

————, and Buckingham, B. R., *Illinois Examination I and II.* Bloomington, Illinois: Public School Publishing Company, 1920.

————, *Illinois General Intelligence Scale.* Bloomington, Illinois: Public School Publishing Company, 1919 (revised, 1920).

————, DeVoss, J. C., and Kelly, F. J., *Educational Tests and Measurements.* Boston: Houghton Mifflin, 1924.

————, et al., *Ten Years of Educational Research: 1918–27.* Urbana, Illinois: University of Illinois, Bureau of Educational Research, Bulletin No. 42, 1928.

Munsterberg, H., "Zur individual psychologie," *Centrbl. Nervenheilk Psychiatrie,* Vol. 14, 1891, pp. 196–198.

Murchison, C., ed., *A History of Psychology in Autobiography,* Volume I. Worcester, Massachusetts: Clark University Press, 1930.

————, *A History of Psychology in Autobiography,* Volume II. Worcester, Massachusetts: Clark University Press, 1932.

————, *A History of Psychology in Autobiography,* Volume III. Worcester, Massachusetts: Clark University Press, 1936.

Murphy, G., *Historical Introduction to Modern Psychology.* New York: Harcourt, Brace, 1950.

Nelson, M. J., Lamke, T. A., and Kelso, P. C., *Henmon-Nelson Tests of Mental Ability, College Edition.* Boston: Houghton Mifflin, 1961.

Norsworthy, Naomi, "The psychology of mentally deficient children." *Archives of Psychology,* No. 1, 1906.

Nunnally, J., Jr., *Tests and Measurements.* New York: McGraw-Hill, 1959.

Odell, C. W., *Conservation of Intelligence in Illinois High Schools.* Urbana, Illinois: University of Illinois, Bureau of Educational Research, Bulletin No. 22, 1925.

Oehrn, A., *Experimentelle Studien zur Individual-Psychologie.* Originally published in 1889. Reprinted in *Psychologie Arbeiten,* Vol. 1, 1895, pp. 92–152.

Otis, A. S., "An absolute point scale for the group measurement of intelligence, Part I." *Journal of Educational Psychology,* Vol. 9, 1918a, pp. 249–261.

————, "An absolute point scale for the group measurement of intelligence, Part II." *Journal of Educational Psychology,* Vol. 9, 1918b, pp. 333–347.

————, *Group Intelligence Scale.* New York: World Book Company, 1918c.

————, *Otis Classification Test.* New York: World Book Company, 1923–1941.

————, *Otis Group Intelligence Scale, Primary Examination.* New York: World Book Company, 1920.

————, *Otis Quick-Scoring Tests of Mental Ability.* New York: World Book Company, 1936–1954.

————, *Otis Self-Administering Tests of Mental Ability, Higher Examination.* New York: World Book Company, 1922a (revised, 1927).

————, *Otis Self-Administering Tests of Mental Ability, Intermediate Examination.* New York: World Book Company, 1922b.

Pearson, K., *The Life, Letters and Labors of Francis Galton.* London: University of Columbia Press, 1914.

————, "On the general theory of the influence of selection of correlation and variation." *Biometrika,* Vol. 8, 1912, pp. 437–443.

————, "On the laws on inheritance in man, II: on the inheritance of the mental and moral characters in man and its comparison with the inheritance of the physical characters." *Biometrika,* Vol. 3, 1904, pp. 131–160.

Peik, W. E., "A generation of research on the curriculum." *Thirty-seventh Yearbook, National Society for the Study of Education,* Vol. 37, 1938, pp. 53–67.

Peterson, J., *Early Conceptions and Tests of Intelligence.* New York: World Book Company, 1925.

Pillsbury, W. B., *The History of Psychology.* New York: Norton, 1929.

Pintner, R., *Intelligence Testing: methods and results.* New York: Henry Holt & Company, 1923 (revised, 1931).

————, "A non-language group intelligence test." *Journal of Applied Psychology,* Vol. 3, 1919, pp. 199–214.

————, *Pintner Mental Educational Survey Test.* Columbus, Ohio: College Book Company, 1921.

————, and Cunningham, Bess V., *Pintner-Cunningham Primary Mental Test.* New York: World Book Company, 1923.

————, and Paterson, D. G., *A Scale of Performance Tests.* New York: Appleton, 1917.

Porteus, S. D., *Guide to Porteus Maze Test.* Vineland, New Jersey: The Training School, 1924.

Postman, L., ed., *Psychology in the Making.* New York: Alfred A. Knopf, 1962.

Pressey, Luella M., *Pressey Mental Survey Tests, Primer Scale.* Bloomington, Illinois: Public School Publishing Company, 1920.

Pressey, S. L., and Pressey, Luella M., "A brief group scale of intelligence for use in school surveys." *Journal of Educational Research,* Vol. 11, 1920, pp. 89–100.

————, "A group point scale for measuring general intelligence, with first results from 1100 school children." *Journal of Applied Psychology,* Vol. 2, 1918, pp. 250–269.

Pressey, S. L., and Richards, R. C., *American History Test.* Bloomington, Illinois: Public School Publishing Company, 1922.

Pressey, S. L., *et al., Diagnostic Tests in English Composition.* Bloomington, Illinois: Public School Publishing Co., 1923.

Proctor, W. M., "The use of psychological tests in the educational guidance of high-school pupils." *Journal of Educational Research,* Vol. 1, 1920a, pp. 369–381.

————, "The use of psychological tests in the vocational guidance of high-school pupils." *Journal of Educational Research,* Vol. 2, 1920b, pp. 533–546.

Rabin, A. I., "The use of the Wechsler-Bellevue scale with normal and abnormal persons." *Psychological Bulletin,* Vol. 42, 1945, pp. 410–422.

Ramul, K., "The problem of measurement in the psychology of the eighteenth century." *American Psychologist,* Vol. 15, 1960, pp. 256–265.

Reisman, J. M., *The Development of Clinical Psychology.* New York: Appleton-Century-Crofts, 1966.

Rice, J. M., "Educational research: causes of success and failure in arithmetic." *Forum,* Vol. 35, 1903a, pp. 437–452.

————, "Educational research: the results of a test in language." *Forum,* Vol. 35, 1903b, pp. 269–293.

————, "Educational research: a test in arithmetic." *Forum,* Vol. 34, 1902, pp. 281–297.

————, "The futility of the spelling grind, I." *Forum,* Vol. 23, 1897a, pp. 163–172.

————, "The futility of the spelling grind, II." *Forum,* Vol. 23, 1897b, pp. 409–419.

————, "Need school be a blight to child life?" *Forum,* Vol. 9, 1891a, pp. 529–535.

————, "The public schools of New York City, I and II." *Epoch,* Vol. 9, 1891b, pp. 390–391, 406–408.

————, *The Public School System of the United States.* New York: Century Company, 1893.

Roback, A. A., *History of Psychology and Psychiatry.* New York: Philosophical Library, 1961.

Rosenblum, Eve, "The development of special education: perceived historically." *Enfance,* Vol. 2, 1961, pp. 165–178.

Ross, C. C., *Measurement in Today's Schools,* 2nd ed. New York: Prentice-Hall, 1947.

Ruch, G. M., "College qualifying examinations." *School and Society,* Vol. 21, 1925, pp. 583–586.

————, *The Improvement of the Written Examination.* Chicago, Illinois: Scott, Foresman and Company, 1924.

————, and Stoddard, G. D., *Tests and Measurements in High School Instruction.* New York: World Book Company, 1927.

————, *et al., Compass Diagnostic Tests in Arithmetic.* Chicago, Illinois: Scott, Foresman and Company, 1925.

————, *Iowa High School Content Examination.* Iowa City, Iowa: State University of Iowa, Bureau of Educational Research and Service, 1923.

Scannell, D. P., *et al., Tests of Academic Progress.* Boston: Houghton Mifflin, 1964.

Scates, D. E., "Fifty years of objective measurement and research in education." *Journal of Educational Research,* Vol. 41, 1947, pp. 241–264.

Scripture, E. W., "Tests on school children." *Educational Research,* Vol. 5, 1893, pp. 52–61.

Seashore, C. E., *The Psychology of Musical Talent.* Boston: Silver Burdett and Company, 1919.

Seguin, E., *Idiocy: its treatment by the physiological method.* Reprinted from the original edition of 1866. New York: Teachers College, Columbia University Bureau of Publications, 1907.

Sharp, Stella, "Individual psychology: a study in psychological method." *American Journal of Psychology,* Vol. 10, 1899, pp. 329–391.

Smith, E. R., and Tyler, R. W., *Appraising and Recording Student Progress.* New York: Harper & Brothers, 1942.

Spearman, C., *The Abilities of Man*. London: Macmillan, 1927.

————, " 'General intelligence' objectively determined and measured." *American Journal of Psychology*, Vol. 15, 1904a, pp. 201–293.

————, *The Nature of 'Intelligence' and the Principles of Cognition*. London: Macmillan, 1923.

————, "The proof and measurement of association between two things." *American Journal of Psychology*, Vol. 15, 1904b, pp. 72–101.

————, "Some issues in the theory of 'g,' " In *British Association, Proceedings, Section J*. Southampton, England: British Association, 1925.

Stanley, J. C., *Measurement in Today's Schools*, 4th ed. Englewood Cliffs, New Jersey: Prentice-Hall, 1964.

Starch, D., *Educational Measurements*. New York: Macmillan, 1916.

————, "The measurements of handwriting." *Journal of Educational Research*, Vol. 4, 1913, pp. 415–418.

————, and Elliott, E. C., "Reliability of grading work in mathematics." *School Review*, Vol. 21, 1913, pp. 254–259.

Stern, A. W., "The nature of g and the concept of intelligence." *Acta Psychologia*, Vol. 12, 1956, pp. 282–289.

Stern, W., *The Psychological Methods of Testing Intelligence*. Translated by G. M. Whipple. Baltimore: Warwick and York, 1914.

————, "The study of individuality." *American Journal of Psychology*, Vol. 21, 1910, pp. 279–282.

————, "The super-normal child." *Journal of Educational Psychology*, Vol. 2, 1911, pp. 143–148, 181–190.

————, "The theory of the constancy of intelligence." *Psychological Clinic*, Vol. 16, 1925, pp. 110–118.

Stone, C. W., *Arithmetical Abilities and Some Factors Determining Them*. New York: Teachers College, Columbia University, 1908.

————, "Problems in the scientific study of the teaching of arithmetic." *Journal of Educational Psychology*, Vol. 4, 1913, pp. 1–16.

Stutsman, Rachel, *Mental Measurement of Preschool Children*. New York: World Book Company, 1931b.

————, *Merrill-Palmer Scale of Mental Tests*. Chicago, Illinois: C. H. Stoelting Company, 1931b.

Sullivan, Elizabeth T., "Psychographic representation of results of the Stanford Revision of the Binet-Simon tests." *Juvenile Delinquency*, Vol. 10, 1926, pp. 284–285.

————, Clark, W. W., and Tiegs, E. W., *California Test of Mental Maturity*. Monterey, California: California Test Bureau, 1936–1963.

Symonds, P. M., *Measurement in Secondary Education*. New York: Macmillan, 1927.

Terman, L. M., *Concept Mastery Test*. New York: The Psychological Corporation, 1956.

————, "Genius and stupidity." *Pedagogical Seminary*, Vol. 13, 1906, pp. 307–373.

————, *The Intelligence of School Children.* Boston: Houghton Mifflin, 1919.

————, *Measurement of Intelligence: an explanation of and a complete guide for the use of the Stanford revision and extension of the Binet-Simon intelligence scale.* Boston: Houghton Mifflin, 1916.

————, "A study of precosity and prematuration." *American Journal of Psychology*, Vol. 16, 1905, pp. 145–183.

————, *Terman Group Test of Mental Ability.* New York: World Book Company, 1920.

————, and Chase, Jessie M., "The psychology, biology and pedagogy of genius." *Psychological Bulletin*, Vol. 17, No. 12, 1920.

————, and Childs, H. G., "A tentative revision and extension of the Binet-Simon measuring scale of intelligence." *Journal of Educational Psychology*, Vol. 3, 1912, pp. 61–74, 133–143, 192–208, 277–289.

————, and McNemar, Q., *Terman-McNemar Test of Mental Ability.* New York: World Book Company, 1941–1949.

————, and Merrill, Maud A., *Measuring Intelligence.* Boston: Houghton Mifflin, 1937.

————, *Stanford-Binet Intelligence Scale: Manual for the Third Revision, Form L-M.* Boston: Houghton Mifflin, 1960.

————, and Oden, Melita H., *Genetic Studies of Genius: IV. The gifted child grows up: twenty-five years' follow-up of a superior group.* Palo Alto, California: Stanford University Press, 1947.

————, *Genetic Studies of Genius: V. The gifted group at mid-life: thirty-five years' follow-up of the superior child.* Palo Alto, California: Stanford University Press, 1959.

————, et al., *Genetic Studies of Genius: I. Mental and physical traits of a thousand gifted children.* Palo Alto, California: Stanford University Press, 1925 (second edition, 1926).

Thomson, G. H., *The Factorial Analysis of Human Ability.* Boston: Houghton Mifflin, 1939.

Thorndike, E. L., "Animal intelligence: an experimental study of the associative processes in animals." *Psychological Review, Monographs Supplement*, Vol. 2, No. 8, 1898.

————, *Animal Intelligence.* New York: Macmillan, 1911.

————, "Educational measurements of fifty years ago." *Journal of Educational Psychology*, Vol. 4, 1913a, pp. 561–562.

————, *Educational Psychology.* New York: Teachers College, Columbia University, 1903.

————, *Educational Psychology: I. the original nature of man.* New York: Teachers College, Columbia University, 1913b.

———, *Educational Psychology: II. the psychology of learning*. New York: Teachers College, Columbia University, 1913c.

———, *Educational Psychology: III. individual differences and their causes*. New York: Teachers College, Columbia University, 1914a.

———, *The Elimination of People from the School*. Washington, D.C.: U.S. Department of the Interior, Bureau of Education, 1907.

———, "An experiment in grading problems in algebra." *Mathematics Teacher*, Vol. 6, 1914b, pp. 123–134.

———, "Handwriting." *Teachers College Record*, Vol. 11, 1910, pp. 83–175.

———, "Improved scale for measuring ability in reading." *Teachers College Record*, Vol. 16, 1915, pp. 445–467.

———, *Intelligence Examination*. New York: T. C. Burroughs, 1918a.

———, *Introduction to The Theory of Mental and Social Measurements*. New York: Teachers College, Columbia University, 1904.

———, "Introduction to the Theory of Social and Mental Measurements, 2nd ed., New York: Teachers College, Columbia University, 1913d.

———, "Measurement in education." *Twenty-first Yearbook, National Society for the Study of Education*, Vol. 21, 1922, pp. 1–9.

———, "Measurement of twins." *Journal of Philosophy, Psychology, and Scientific Method*, Vol. 2, 1905, pp. 547–553.

———, "Mental fatigue." *Psychological Review*, Vol. 7, 1900, pp. 466–482, 547–579.

———, "The nature, purposes and general methods of measurements of educational products," *Seventeenth Yearbook, National Society for the Study of Education*, Vol. 17, 1918b, pp. 16–24.

———, "The new psychological tests." *Educational Review*, February, 1920.

———, "Notes on the significance and use of the Hillegas scale for measuring the quality of English composition." *English Journal*, Vol. 2, 1913e, pp. 551–561.

———, *Principles of Teaching*. New York: Teachers College, Columbia University, 1906.

———, *Thorndike's Scale Alpha 2 for Measuring the Understanding of Sentences*. New York: Bureau of Publications, Teachers College, Columbia University, 1916.

———, and Fox, W., *Relation between the Different Abilities in the Study of Arithmetic*. (*Columbia University Contributions to Education*.) New York: Teachers College, Columbia University, 1903.

———, and Woodworth, R. S., "Influence of improvement in one mental function upon efficiency of other mental functions." *Psychological Review*, Vol. 8, 1901, pp. 247–261.

———, Lay, W., and Dean, P. R., "The relation of accuracy in sensory discrimination of general intelligence." *American Journal of Psychology*, Vol. 20, 1909, pp. 364–369.

————, Woodyard, Ella, and Lorge, I., "Four new forms of the I.E.R. Intelligence Scale for use on the college and higher levels." *School and Society*, Vol. 42, 1935, pp. 271–272.

————, *et al., The Measurement of Intelligence.* New York: Teachers College, Columbia University, Bureau of Publications, 1927.

Thurstone, L. L., "Autobiography." In E. G. Boring, *et al.*, eds., *A History of Psychology in Autobiography*, Volume IV. Worcester, Massachusetts: Clark University Press, 1952, pp. 295–321.

————, "A cycle-omnibus test for college students." *Journal of Educational Research*, Vol. 4, 1921, pp. 265–278.

————, "The learning curve equation." *Psychological Monographs*, Vol. 26, No. 3, 1919a.

————, "Multiple factor analysis." *Psychological Review*, Vol. 38, 1931, pp. 406–427.

————, *Multiple Factor Analysis.* Chicago, Illinois: University of Chicago Press, 1947.

————, *Primary Mental Abilities.* Chicago, Illinois: University of Chicago Press, Psychometric Monograph No. 1., 1938.

————, *Psychological Examination for College Freshmen.* Pittsburgh, Pennsylvania: Carnegie Institute of Technology, 1919b.

————, *Theory of Mental Tests.* Chicago, Illinois: University of Chicago Press, 1925.

————, *Theory of Multiple Factors.* Chicago, Illinois: University of Chicago Press, 1933.

————, *Vectors of the Mind: multiple-factor analysis for the isolation of primary traits.* Chicago, Illinois: University of Chicago Press, 1935.

————, and Thurstone, Thelma G., *American Council on Education Psychological Examination for College Freshmen.* Washington, D.C.: American Council on Education, 1925–1947. Princeton, New Jersey: Educational Testing Service, 1947–1954.

————, *American Council on Education Psychological Examination for High School Students.* Washington, D.C.: American Council on Education, 1933–1947.

Tiegs, E. W., and Clark, W. W., *California Achievement Tests.* Monterey, California: California Test Bureau, 1936–1963.

————, *Progressive Achievement Tests.* Monterey, California: California Test Bureau, 1933.

Toops, H. A., *Ohio State University Psychological Test.* Columbus, Ohio: Ohio College Association, 1919–1958.

Tsao, F., "Is the AQ or F score the last word in determining individual effort?" *Journal of Educational Psychology*, Vol. 34, 1943, pp. 513–526.

Tuddenham, R. D., "The nature and measurement of intelligence." In L. G. Postman, ed., *Psychology in the Making: histories of selected research problems.* New York: Alfred A. Knopf, 1962, pp. 469–525.

Tyler, Leona E., *Psychology of Human Differences,* 3rd ed. New York: Appleton-Century-Crofts, 1965.

Tyler, R., "The specific techniques of investigation: examining and testing acquired knowledge, skill and ability." *Thirty-seventh Yearbook of the National Society for the Study of Education.* Bloomington, Illinois: Public School Publishing Company, Vol. 37, 1938, pp. 341–355.

U.S. Department of the Army, TAGO, Personnel Research Branch. "The Army General Classification Test." *Psychological Bulletin,* Vol. 42, 1945, pp. 760–768.

Van Wagenen, M. J., *English Composition Scales.* New York: World Book Company, 1923.

Vaughn, K. W., *et al., Iowa Tests of Educational Development.* Chicago, Illinois: Science Research Associates, 1942–1963.

Walker, Helen M., "What the tests do not test." *The Mathematics Teacher,* Vol. 18, 1925, pp. 45–53.

Watson, R. L., *The Great Psychologists: from Aristotle to Freud.* New York: J. B. Lippincott, 1963.

Wechsler, D., *Manual for the Wechsler Adult Intelligence Scale.* New York: The Psychological Corporation, 1955.

————, *The Measurement and Appraisal of Adult Intelligence,* 4th ed. Baltimore, Maryland: Williams and Wilkins, 1958.

————, *The Measurement of Adult Intelligence.* Baltimore, Maryland: Williams and Wilkins, 1939.

————, *Wechsler Intelligence Scale for Children, Manual.* New York: The Psychological Corporation, 1949.

————, *Wechsler Preschool and Primary Scale of Intelligence.* New York: The Psychological Corporation, 1967.

Wells, F. L., "Alternative methods for mental examiners." *Journal of Applied Psychology,* Vol. 1, 1917, pp. 134–143.

Whipple, G. M., *Classes for Gifted Children.* Bloomington, Illinois: Public School Publishing Company, 1919a.

————, *Group tests for grammar grades.* Bloomington, Illinois: Public School Publishing Company, 1919b.

————, "The national intelligence tests." *Journal of Educational Research,* Vol. 4, 1921, pp. 16–31.

————, "A range of information test." *Psychological Review,* Vol. 16, 1909, pp. 347–361.

————, "Vocabulary and word-building tests." *Psychological Review,* Vol. 15, 1908, pp. 94–105.

————, and Whipple, H. D., *Illinois general intelligence scale.* Bloomington, Illinois: Public School Publishing Company, 1926.

Winkler, J. K., and Brumberg, W., *Mind Explorers.* New York: Reynal and Hitchcock, 1939.

Wissler, C., "The correlation of mental and physical traits." *Psychological Monographs*, Vol. 3, 1901, pp. 1–62.

Witham, E. C., "School and teacher measurement." *Journal of Educational Psychology*, Vol. 5, 1914a, pp. 267–278.

———, "School measurement." *Journal of Educational Psychology*, Vol. 5, 1914b, pp. 571–588.

Witty, P. A., and Lehman, H. C., "The instinct hypothesis vs. the maturation hypothesis." *Psychological Review*, Vol. 40, 1933, pp. 33–59.

Wood, B. D., *Measurement in Higher Education*. New York: The World Book Company, 1923.

Woodruff, A. D., and Pritchard, M. W., "Some trends in the development of psychological tests." *Educational and Psychological Measurements*, Vol. 9, 1949, pp. 105–108.

Woodworth, R. S., *Contemporary Schools of Psychology*. New York: The Ronald Press Company, 1948.

Woody, C., *et al.*, "A symposium on the effects of measurement on instruction." *Journal of Educational Research*, Vol. 28, 1935, pp. 481–527.

Wundt, W., *Beiträge zur theorie der sinneswahrnehmung*. Lepizig and Heidelberg: C. F. Winter, 1862.

———, *Grundzüge der physiologischen psychologie*. Leipzig: Englemann, 1874.

———, *An Introduction to Psychology*, 2nd German ed. Translated by R. Pintner. New York: Macmillan, 1912.

———, *Outlines of Psychology*, 7th revision, German ed. Translated by C. H. Judd. Leipzig: Englemann, 1907.

Wylie, A. T., "A brief history of mental tests." *Teachers College Record*, Vol. 23, 1922, pp. 19–33.

Yerkes, R. M., ed., "Psychological examination of the soldier." In *The Harvey Lectures*. Philadelphia and London: J. B. Lippincott, 1920, pp. 181–215.

———, *Psychological Examining in the United States Army*. (*Memoirs of the National Academy of Sciences*, Volume 15.) Washington, D.C.: U.S. Government Printing Office, 1921.

———, Bridges, J. W., and Hardwick, R. S., *A Point Scale for Measuring Mental Ability*. Baltimore, Maryland: Warwick and York, 1915.

Yoakum, C. S., and Yerkes, R. M., eds., *Army Mental Tests*. New York: Henry Holt and Company, 1920.

Young, K., "The history of mental testing." *The Pedagogical Seminary*, Vol. 31, 1923, pp. 1–48.

Zilboorg, G., and Henry, G. W., *A History of Medical Psychology*. New York: Norton, 1941.

INDEX

Tyler, R. W., 83
Vaughn, K. W., 84
Vincent, Leona E., 63
Viteles, M. S., 54
Weber, E., 4
Wechsler, D., 67 ff.
Wells, F. L., 42 ff.
Whipple, G. M., 41 ff., 47, 55–56, 72

Wissler, C., 11
Witty, P. A., 77
Wood, B. D., 81
Woodworth, R. S., 24–25, 35, 42 ff., 71
Wundt, W., 5–6, 8–9, 32
Yerkes, R. M., 41 ff., 49, 53, 56
Yoakum, C. S., 47–48, 53, 72

28-202